# The Architecture of Point William: A Laboratory for Living

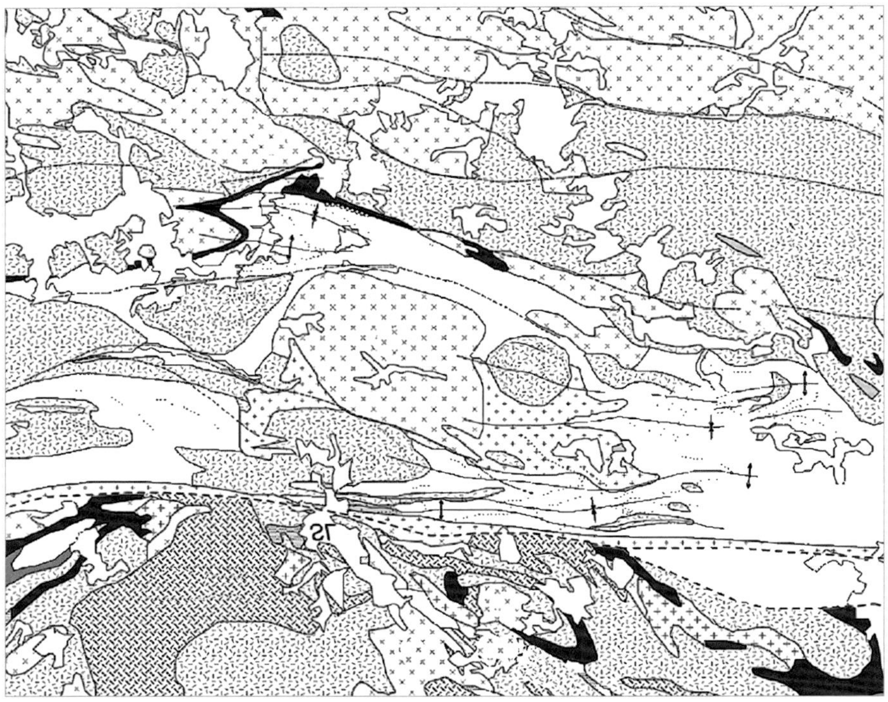

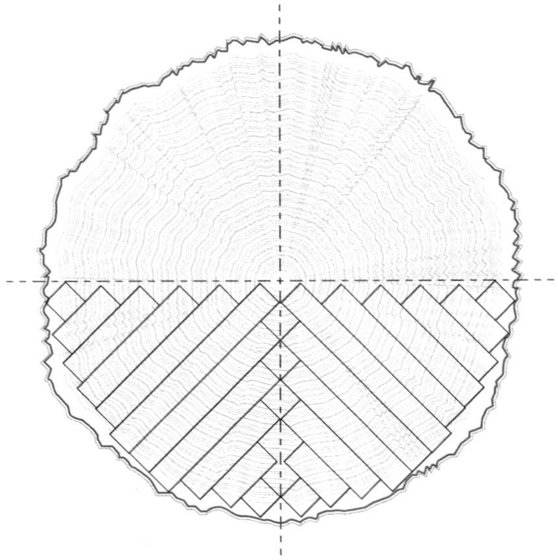

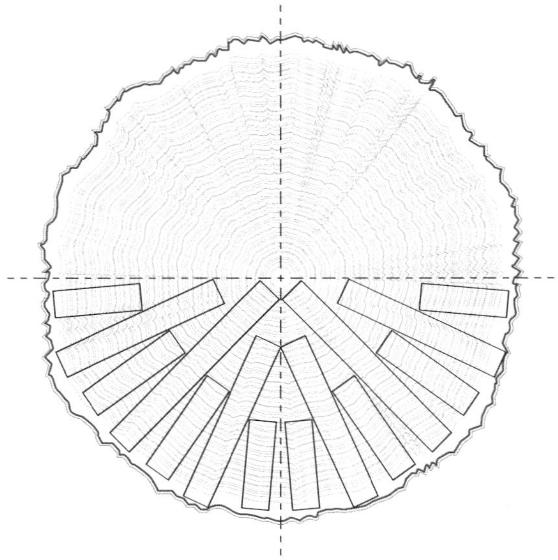

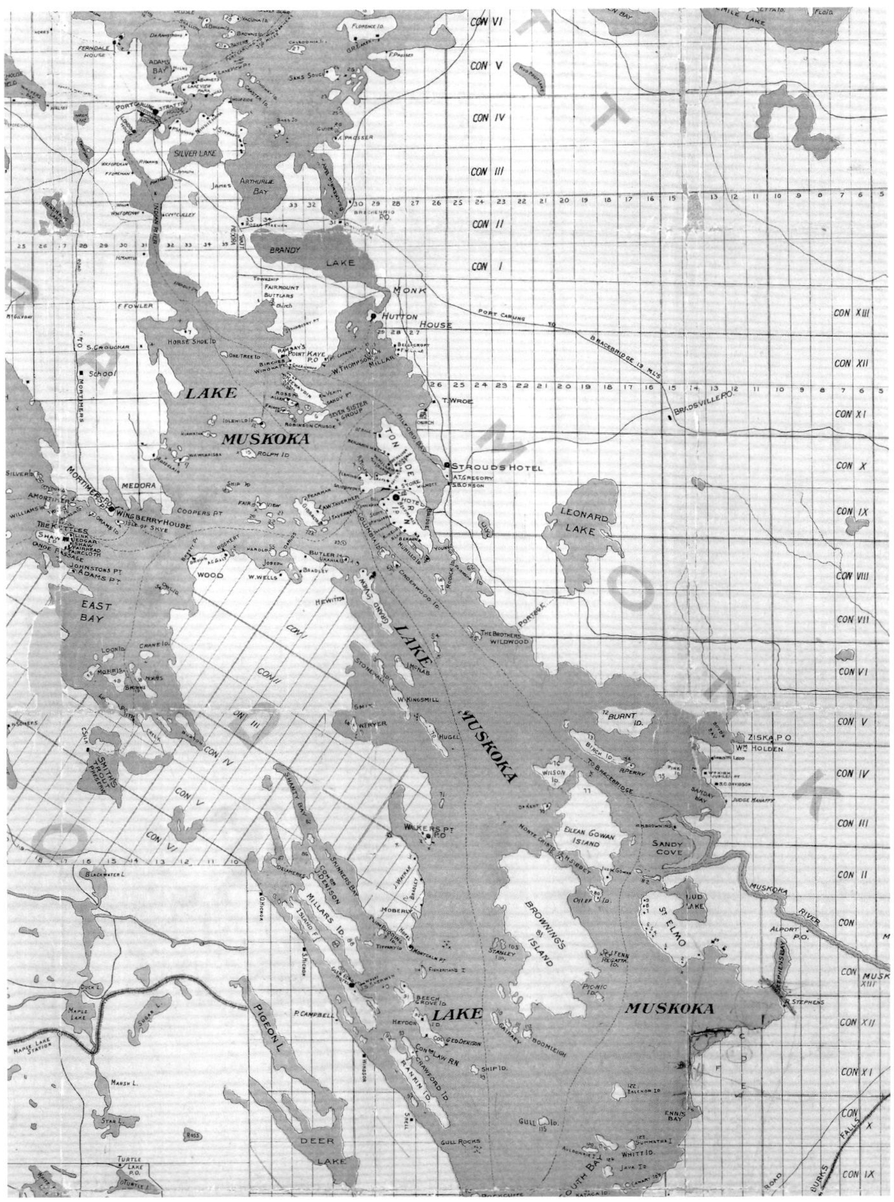
LAKE MUSKOKA
LAKE
MUSKOKA
LAKE MUSKOKA
LAKE
MUSKOKA
BRANDY LAKE
SILVER LAKE
ARTHURLE BAY
MONK
HUTTON HOUSE
STROUDS HOTEL
LEONARD LAKE
EAST BAY
MEDORA
WINDBERRY HOUSE
COOPERS PT
WOOD
W. WELLS
BURNT ID.
ZISKA P.O.
W. HOLDEN
ELEAN GOWAN ISLAND
SANDY COVE
BROWNING'S ISLAND
ST ELMO
MUSKOKA RIVER
ALPORT P.O.
MILLARS ID.
MOBERLY
PIGEON L
P. CAMPBELL
DEER LAKE
MAPLE LAKE
TURTLE LAKE P.O.
WALKERS PT
SHIP ID.
GULL ROCKS
WHITE ID.
SOUTH BAY
CON VI
CON V
CON IV
CON III
CON II
CON I
CON XIII
CON XII
CON XI
CON X
CON IX
CON VIII
CON VII

# Table of Contents

# Foreword

It seems like only yesterday that Brigitte Shim and Howard Sutcliffe came to Point William for the first time. In fact, it was almost 25 years ago—two and a half decades during which this remarkable couple became not only our partners, but our close friends. As the four of us walked the Muskoka site that autumn afternoon, and later sat on a promontory overlooking the lake, little did we anticipate the long, often challenging, but richly rewarding journey on which we were about to embark.

When we began, Shim-Sutcliffe was still a relatively young firm, trying to gain traction at the highest, most demanding level of architectural practice. Although its portfolio of work was then modest in volume, one thing was clear: it was uncompromising about excellence. A very high standard of design, sensitivity to building in harmony with nature, scrupulous attention to every last detail, and meticulous concern for execution—all of this was apparent, and resonated deeply with us.

In time Brigitte and Howard would earn plaudits for Integral House in Toronto; the Wong Dai Sin Temple in Markham, Ontario; Congregation Bet Ha'am Synagogue in Portland, Maine; and the residence and chapel for the Sisters of St. Joseph in Toronto. Shim-Sutcliffe are currently working on projects in Moscow, Hong Kong and Honolulu.

Today, the firm's name, Shim-Sutcliffe Architects, is often mentioned in conversations about outstanding modern architecture. Their metrics for performance are unchanged: nothing leaves their studio without Brigitte's and Howard's personal imprimatur. Their skills are complementary. As another justly celebrated Canadian architect, Bruce Kuwabara, said of them, "Brigitte is the face and the voice, and Howard is the hand and the eye. It's a perfect symbiosis."

Kuwabara is far from alone in his respect for and appreciation of their work. The distinguished architectural historian Kenneth Frampton came twice to walk the Point William property. Each time, he left shaking his head at what had been achieved here.

As with many things in life, the Point William development was largely serendipitous. We initially asked Brigitte and Howard to design a new boathouse. When that was complete, they re-imagined the outdoor fire pit and a few other smaller features on the property. All of these were realized at such a high level that, when we later decided to build a new guest cottage, a new main cottage, and finally a new garage, we knew that each of these would have to match the very high bar that had already been set. From the earliest improvements—the stone wall that marks the site's entry point, to the last, a platform that catches the late afternoon sun—every decision led almost inevitably to the next.

We feel privileged to have spent the time we did with Brigitte and Howard. At every stage, they welcomed our input. Inevitably, there were differences of opinion about process or design, but in every instance, our discussions opened doors—never closed them.

No less critically, Brigitte and Howard embraced the advice of the local craftspeople who were charged with realizing their vision. From the outset, it was important that the work express the distinct local vernacular, a resonance that could only be achieved by absorbing the accumulated wisdom and experience of the local trades.

Living at Point William amazes and delights us still. Scarcely a day goes by that we do not comment upon it, not only upon the obvious beauty in which we are enveloped, but the fulfillment of what we always regarded as the essential purpose—to create a warm and inviting point of connection for our family and friends. That, in the end, is the miracle of Brigitte and Howard's achievement. What they produced exceeded our highest expectations, in terms of design and execution. It also did what excellent architecture should always strive for, to create an environment that transcends physical space and elevates the human dimension.

—Gerald Sheff and Shanitha Kachan

# Architects' Note

One autumn day in 1996, we sat with our clients, Gerald Sheff and Shanitha Kachan, on the rocky shore of Lake Muskoka and discussed the possibilities of the property they were contemplating purchasing. Twenty-four years later, we are documenting the results of that extended journey of design in this book. During that process we had the opportunity to establish a rich dialogue between found conditions, new interventions, and a reimagined landscape on a remarkable site of mixed hardwoods, conifers, and the granite of the Canadian Shield.

Point William is the name given to this slender property jutting out into Lake Muskoka, Ontario, Canada. The material palette of the site, forest, rock, and water combined with the rich history of Muskoka culture—cabins, grand Victorian cottages, and sleek, mahogany lake cruisers—created a deep background that we embraced, celebrated, and reinvented in the designs for this project.

For each portion of the overall Point William project, we responded to a pre-existing condition and developed each building relative to what came before and what might come later. The resonance between the found conditions, the new interventions, and their constant dialogue contributes to the unusual nature of the project. Our design work on this project was not continuous. Since there were large passages of time between design activities, other projects in our studio also influenced our response to successive projects at Point William and, reciprocally, the explorations in this project influenced other work in our studio.

We are presenting the work chronologically by building to capture not only the buildings themselves, but also the spaces and relationships between buildings and the landscape where they are situated. This project became a laboratory for experiments at many scales simultaneously, with explorations in architectural language, furniture, lighting, hardware, and landscape. Each experiment echoes within each project and between the four buildings on the site. Each scale of design, from the door handles to the shaped ceiling, contributes to the rich, spatial experience that weaves together inside and out.

We have been fortunate as architects to work with many exceptional clients, and perhaps none were more engaged in the process of design and its development than Shanitha Kachan and Gerald Sheff. From the first project for the boathouse, the aspiration, commitment, patience, and alignment of values was established, continued, and evolved across the entire project. The pleasure of construction with all its facets, complexities, and challenges was embraced by the clients and the architects. We were also fortunate to work with a remarkable group of highly-skilled and talented builders, craftspeople, and tradespeople, and the results are a credit to all of their considerable efforts.

—Brigitte Shim and Howard Sutcliffe

WRIGHT
WRIGHT

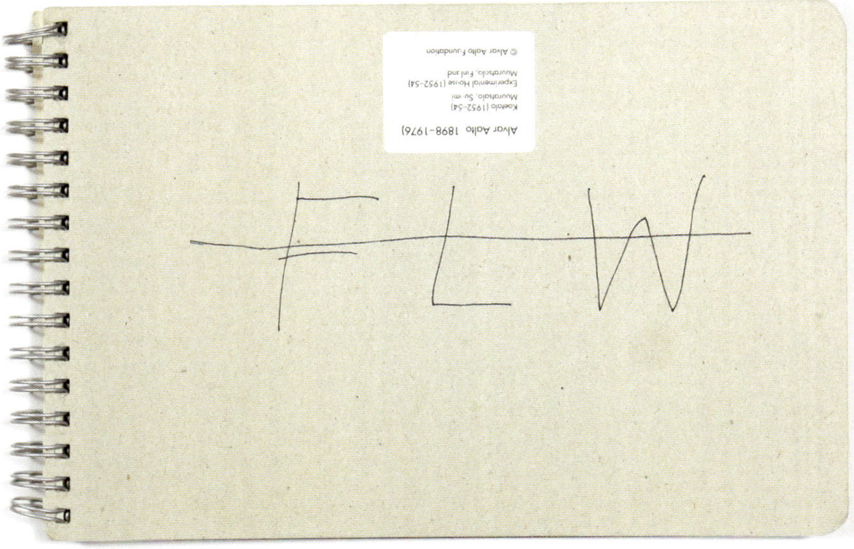

*Kenneth Frampton's sketchbook from his visit to Point William in September 2017.*
*All of the sketches shown in this essay are from Frampton's Point William sketchbook.*

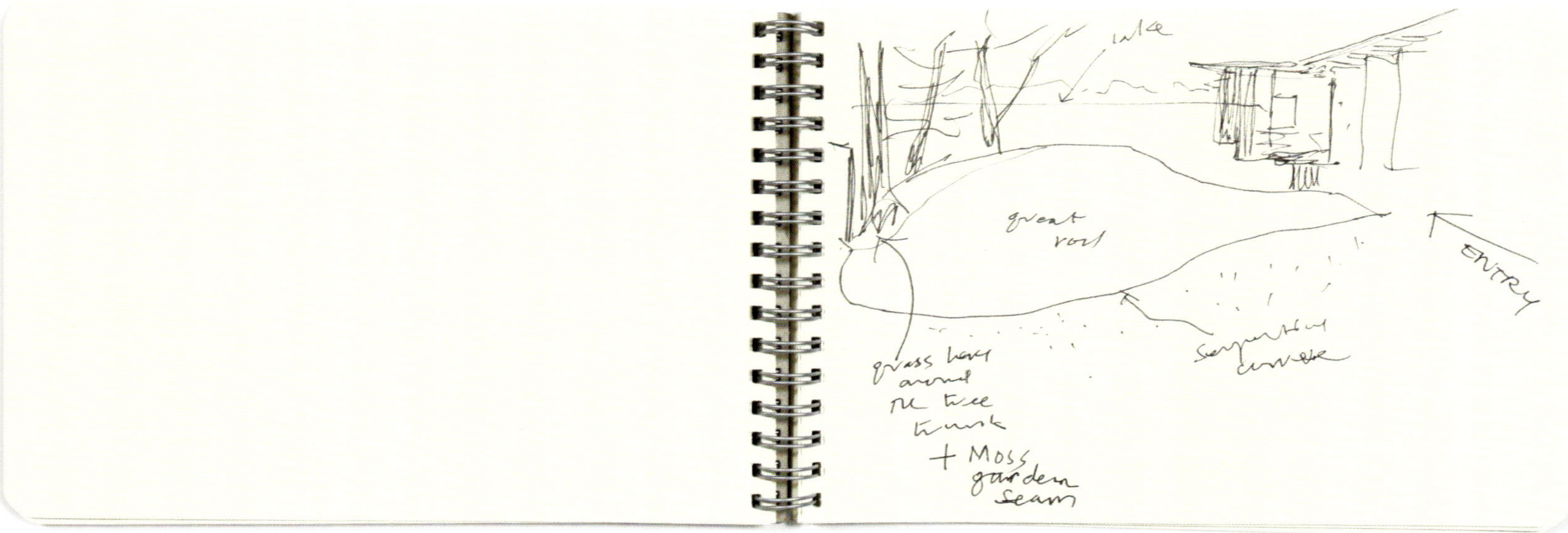
ENTRY
+ Moss
garden
seam

# At Point William

Kenneth Frampton

*Cover of Kenneth Frampton's personal copy of Le Corbusier's Vers une architecture.*

There is something interstitially kinetic about the compound at Point William. Not only are the carefully constructed views reciprocally framed and re-framed by each successive building, but the role of the primary volumes within each structure serve to bracket their mutually asymmetrical interrelationship in such a way as to give the whole a surprisingly cinematic character. This experiential dynamic is suggested by the multiple photographs of the complex taken from different unexpected vantage points, both inside and out, so as to emphasize the metamorphosis of the buildings under different climatic conditions. This imbues each structure with its own volatile, figurative character, which is perennially transformed by the time of day and the ever-changing intensity and angle of light. These dynamic, cubistic exercises in style remind one of Auguste Choisy's foreshortened representation of the Athenian Acropolis as prominently featured in Le Corbusier's *Vers une architecture* of 1923. This testifies to the influence on successive generations of architects throughout the world. That Shim-Sutcliffe is not immune to this all-pervasive, time-honored influence explains an underlying paradox pervading this Canadian retreat. Although it may be read as an exercise in Nordic vernacular modernism, a modernist tour-de-force, it is nonetheless pervaded by a sensibility that has an unmistakably Mediterranean character.

This dynamic, transcending feeling of the picturesque owes much to the undulating contours of the site as it falls toward Lake Muskoka, intermittently interrupted by deeply embedded rocks that check the descent of the land toward the water. Within the topography, this compound is laid out like an oriental stroll garden, wherein each successive structure is conceived in relation to the one that preceded it. At the same time, the surface of the ground has been rendered as a palimpsest, beginning with the soft-brown wood chips underfoot that greet one on arrival by car. Here, while momentarily sheltered by parking bays laid out in chevron formation to the right of the entry, one first encounters the tectonic leitmotif of the entire compound. This takes the form of shoulder-height boxes made out of pre-rusted steel sheets, with each box housing stacked logs of standard length that vary slightly in diameter. Ostensibly provided for the storage of firewood, this feature alludes to Canada's pioneering past and instills the guest cottage and garage with something from another moment in history. Shim-Sutcliffe first used this rustic motif in their Glen Lowry house built to their designs at Lake Memphremagog in 2007.

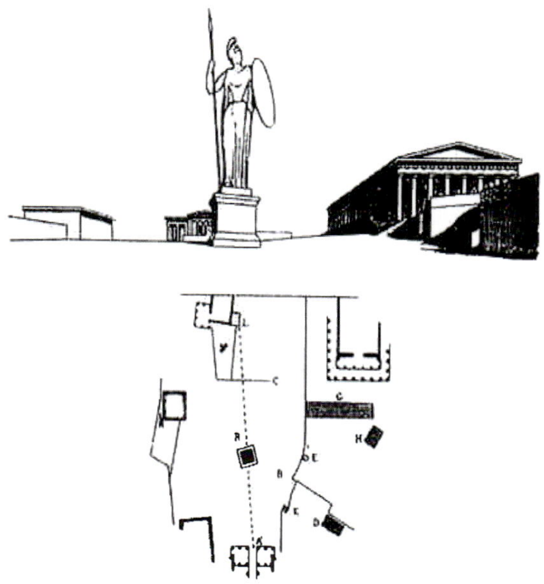

*First View of the Acropolis, August Choisy from Histoire de l'Architecture. Paris Gauthier Villars. Page 415, Vol. 1.*

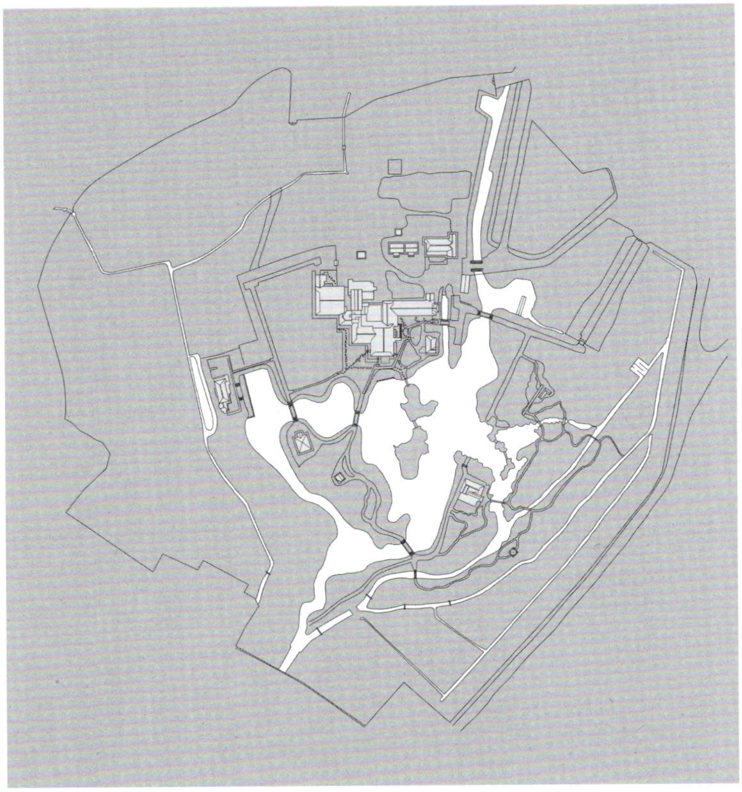

*Site plan of Katsura-Rikyu stroll garden, Kyoto, Japan.*

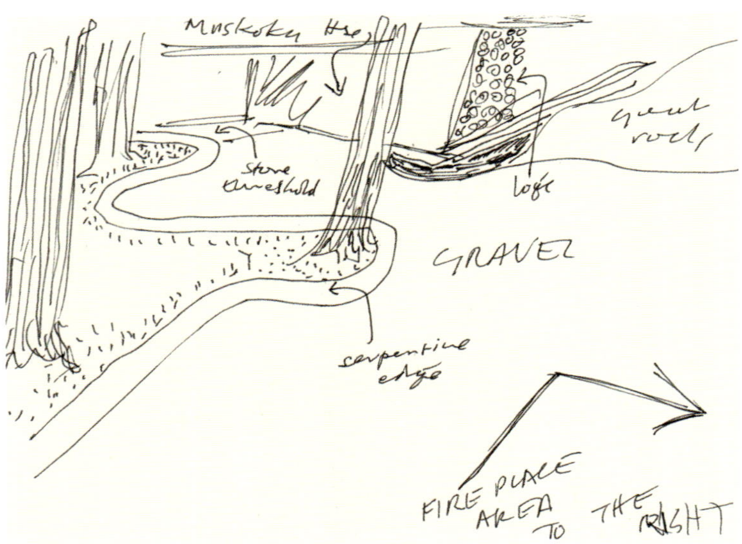


On the upper part of the site, a serpentine walkway of fine-grained, dark-gray gravel, edged by weathering steel and a flat stone wall, unfolds as a unifying overture before the prospect of the entire compound. As this promenade swerves deftly to avoid the trunks of existing trees, it is intercepted early on by a concrete staircase that promises to lead the visitor down to a lower level. It subsequently links to a narrow timber walkway suspended just above the ground, which eventually leads the visitor to the boathouse at the far corner of the site. After completing its initial sweep, the gravel path suddenly terminates before the impediment of the largest embedded rock on the site. At this junction the aforementioned causeway prompts one's movement into three different directions; either one advances directly toward the cottage immediately ahead, or one turns right into the fire pit area, or one swerves left toward the guest cottage, stepping down as one does so, not only by way of accessing the entry to the cottage itself, but also bypassing the guest cottage to enter upon another timber walkway, giving way after a few steps to a winding path that terminates once again in the boathouse. Echoing the finish of the gravel causeway, the fire pit area is also covered with fine-grained, dark-gray granite. At the same time, it is bounded by timber sleepers in order to focus the arena, which are framed by four rough-cut slabs of stone.

The boathouse, the first building to be erected on the site in 1997-1999, rises for two floors above a deck built out of ipe, a South American exotic wood, and affords direct access to the lake. Conceived as a "placeform" within the continuity of the stroll garden, the dock

1 entry drive
2 stacked firewood walls
3 parking
4 garage
5 lawn
6 fire pit
7 cottage
8 rock
9 guest cottage
10 boathouse

*Site plan, Point William.*

is designed to accommodate a large number of people, and is equipped with a bar and a barbeque. A straight timber stair rises from the dock to access the weekend living accommodation on the first floor of the boathouse, where it is suspended above two boat slips, with each slip sheltering a motor launch. This retreat includes a living room and two elevated decks overlooking the lake plus a fairly luxurious bedroom/bathroom suite. A spiraling clockwise circulation leads from the foyer at the top of the straight stair, from where one passes both a kitchenette and a living room before passing to a bedroom, and then a bathroom with a large shower stall and twin wash basins set into a countertop below a long window facing northeast. Among the more atypical features of the boathouse is a half-concealed, Japanese moss garden suspended at the head of the stair. This typically earth-bound element is a surprising feature to be elevated to the first floor, as is the equally audacious hearth and chimney shaft plastered to appear as a single form and set adjacent to the corner window of the living room overlooking the lake.

Sitting beneath a double-pitched, zinc roof, the boathouse is rendered as an articulate timber construction comprised of a hierarchy of exposed rafters, which are capped by closely centered wooden battens or, alternatively, by narrow-boarded timber ceilings that rise up, here and there, into the apex of the roof. The whole is treated as if it were a gigantic piece of finely wrought cabinetwork deconstructed in places to reveal the manner of its fabrication. Within this montage there are subtle allusions to various architects: to Frank Lloyd Wright in general and to the tectonic gestures of Carlo Scarpa and Alvar Aalto in particular. Scarpa is most dramatically referenced through highly elaborate bearings at the top and bottom of four tapering timber posts that support a steel beam fronting onto the dock. Aalto is more discreetly alluded to in the proportions of the timber-framed fenestration. At the same time, the architects make a deft and direct allusion to the Canadian blockhouse tradition, most evident here in the log cabin enclosure of the boat slips.

*Water elevation and interior view. Graphite on paper. A. H. Sutcliffe.*

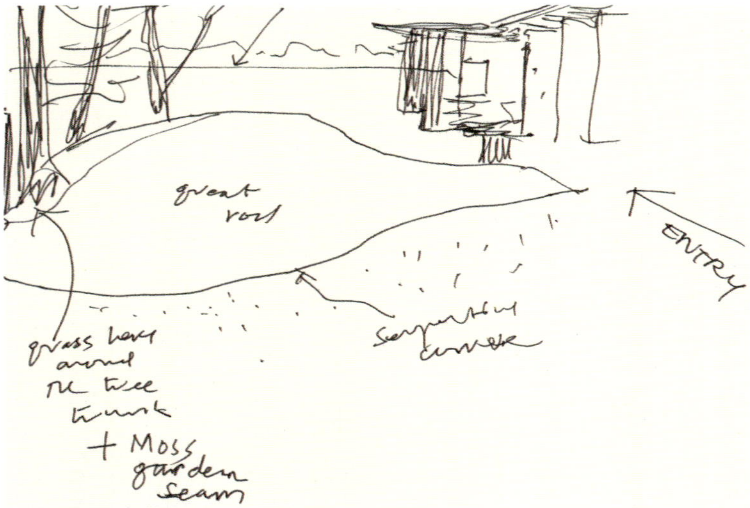

great roof
ENTRY
+ Moss garden seam

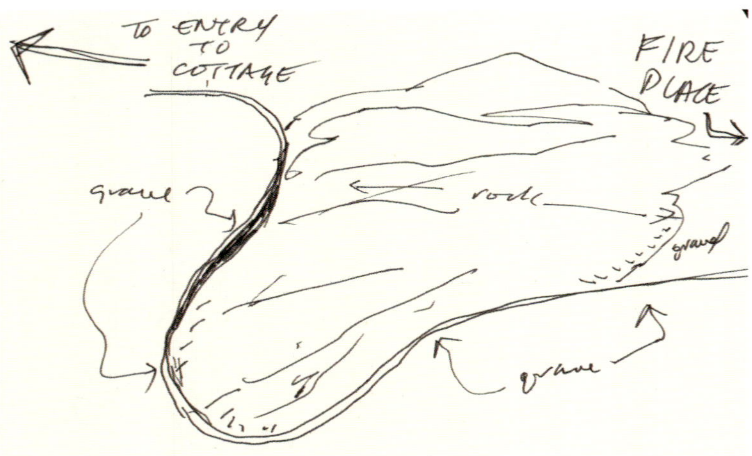

TO ENTRY TO COTTAGE
FIRE PLACE
gravel
rock

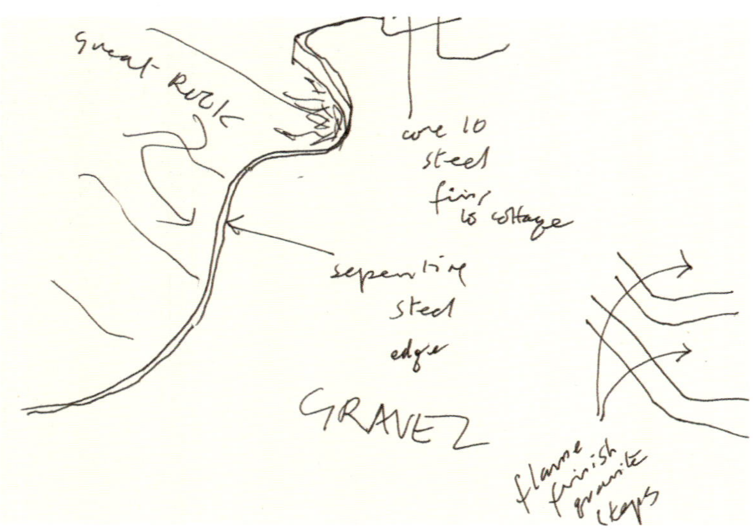

steel
edge
GRAVEL

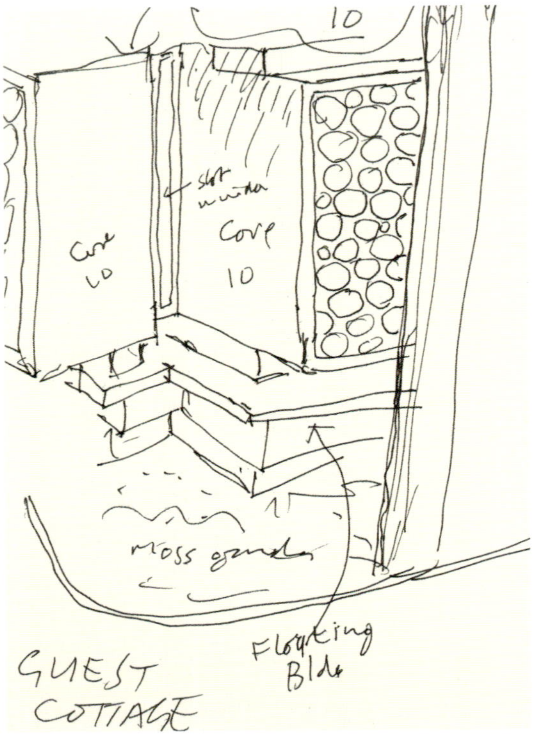

GUEST COTTAGE
Floating Bldg
moss garden
Core 10
slot window

The second building to be realized is the so-called guest cottage in 2007-2010. It replaces a preexisting, traditional Muskoka cabin from 1910 located on virtually the same site and is a simulacrum of pre-rusted, weathering steel. The guest cottage was clad throughout in steel sheet with precisely welded corners, except for the narrow shiplapped planks in weathering steel that cover the gables, sides, and ends, much in the manner of Richard Norman Shaw's Queen Anne style that was perfected in the UK in the second half of the nineteenth century. As with the garage, built in 2015-2018, the guest house is flanked on its sides by steel boxes packed with logs.

Like the boathouse, the guest cottage features spiraling circulation, but now the movement is in an anti-clockwise direction. On entering the guest cottage one passes a diminutive kitchen with a long, countertop window facing the larger cottage. One then enters into a belvedere space equipped with full-height plate glass, timber-framed windows looking toward the lake that orient the entire structure toward the boathouse. This brightly lit space serves as a prelude to the living room located within the depth of the plan and is focused about a monumental chimney breast. A thin, cantilevered stone slab juts out from this mass and intercepts the initial landing of a steel stair with timber treads that rise behind the chimney to the first floor, a mannerist gesture that recalls the cascading stair in Scarpa's Olivetti showroom of 1958.

The ground-floor reinforced-concrete slab of the guest cottage cantilevers out on all four sides to give the impression that the structure floats above the site as the land swirls down to the lake. A band of fine-grained, black granite covers the ground around the perimeter of the cottage like a permanent shadow and corresponds to the extent of the eaves, but it is absent beneath the steel stair cantilevering beyond the body of the building. The thrust of this stair emphasizes the pinwheeling character of the overall form, which assumes a dramatically different aspect from the symmetrical front. As already remarked, the full-height glazing of the belvedere adds to the pinwheel effect as the building turns to the boathouse; this pivoting gesture is further emphasized by the precipitous slope of the ground.

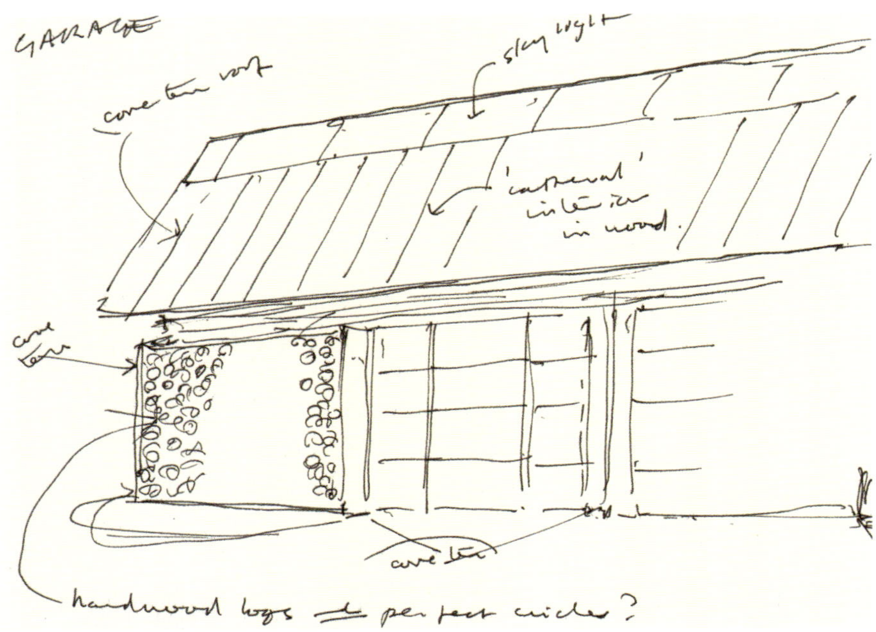

Subject to the same all-enveloping, pre-rusted steel revetment, the garage was the last structure to be erected on the site. The dualist, symmetrical form of this building is initiated by a pair of "up and over" doors emphasized by steel "log" boxes positioned on either side of the doors. The garage has a pitched roof covered with weathering steel, the surface of which is articulated with standing seams. This roof is supported by elaborate timber roof trusses that nostalgically evoke the feeling of a stable, although it is horsepower rather than horses that find shelter within. As with the guest cottage, the gable ends of the building are faced with narrow boards of weathering steel that again allude to the Queen Anne manner.

The entrance to the larger cottage is accompanied by two large field stone walls of differing height, which serve to define at the gable ends what is, in effect, the largest building on the site. The cottage is entered via two large granite steps that give onto the entrance door, and then into to the foyer leading into the main body of the house.

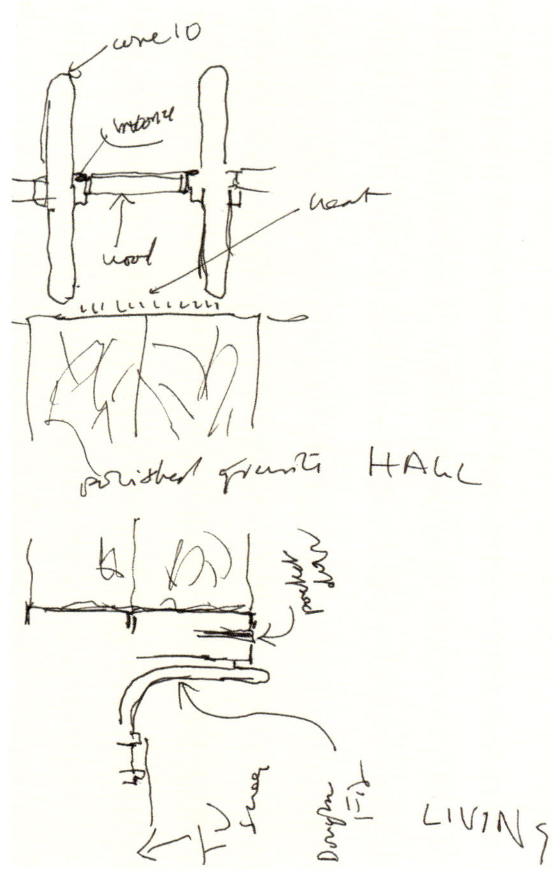
polished granite
HALL
LIVING

made out of a single stainless steel pressing, complete with recessed sinks and draining surfaces. An equally generous feature is the open shelving above the counter-top, backed by a band of continuous fenestration facing southeast.

One of the most exposed spaces of the cottage is the dining room, which not only opens directly onto the living space but also features a plate glass window with re-entrant corners overlooking the lake. The living room is handled as one large glazed partition where rounded glass corners serve to continue the hermetic feeling of the space. This organic sense of enclosure is further emphasized by an undulating timber ceiling that caps the double-height volume. The upper part of this space is pierced by a square clerestory, the glazing of which is screened by vertical timber louvers, inside and out.

Alternations in the basic floor finish pass from granite to oak, and vice-versa, and are continued throughout with similar connotations: granite is used for the more public areas, particularly in the family room at the lower level. The room opens out onto the original rockface of the site. An atypical element at this level is the internal stair linking the ground and lower ground floors and inflecting inward for the last five threads. This organic gesture seems to have been introduced to accommodate additional storage against the north-eastern retaining wall of the lower floor. The swerving of the stair afforded the architects an occasion to showcase a theatrical treatment of the timber balustrading.

The more one contemplates the horizontal thrust of the cottage with its crowning form jutting out toward the lake, the more one is reminded of the horizontal emphasis of Wright's Prairie Style, particularly as this manifested itself most decisively in his Robie House, Chicago, of 1909. At Point William we have much the same formal stress on the main living floor, reinforced in this instance by sharp steel cornices overhanging the northeastern and southwestern elevations. This profile continues around the head of the building, culminating in an extra-deep cornice extending from the face of the kitchen in order to cover the barbeque and counter serving the main deck.

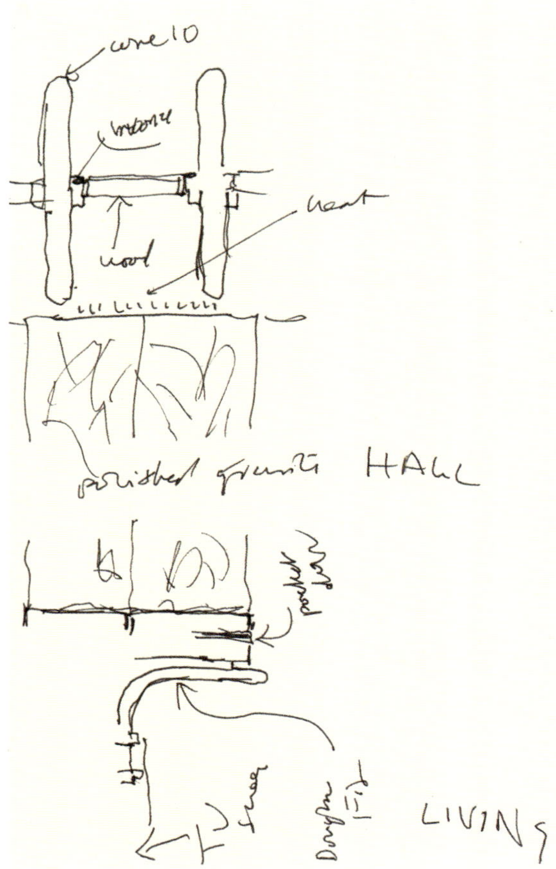
HALL
LIVING

Determined by a four-foot grid, this space is modulated by a syncopated arrangement of fins in pre-rusted steel projecting to an equal degree both within and without the full height of the plate glass fenestration.

Beginning with a single, free-standing fin that establishes the hierarchical rhythm of the entry space, the fins that follow are spaced out according to a modular pattern of 3, 2, 7, 3, with the final three modules corresponding to the width of the family room in the center of the cottage. The floor of this entrance hall is surfaced throughout in Canadian granite with a so-called "leather" finish, which is continued throughout the dining room plus kitchen, study, storage, and finally the floor of the bathroom to the master bedroom. A significant exception to this granite surface is the boarded oak floor of the family room, which gives this part of the house a warmer tone and is echoed in the master dressing room and the three bedrooms located on the ground floors.

The atmosphere of a luxury liner permeates this cottage at every level in part due to the use of rounded re-entrant corners, irrespective of whether these are applied to solid surfaces or to glass enclosures. The resulting quasi-maritime character is additionally emphasized by the use of sliding pocket doors, above all in the family room where such doors cut off this space from the foyer. Single sliding pocket doors are also installed to separate the kitchen from the master bedroom and, similarly, the dining room from the kitchen. Rounded internal corners are ubiquitous on the ground floor, a feature that assumes a particularly hermetic character in the master bedroom where carved, rounded profiles in stone are applied to all the four corners of the space. Significantly there are no such corners in the workaday world of the kitchen, possibly to enhance the aura of efficiency emanating from its free-standing stove top. Equally liberative in character, given the large size of the kitchen, is the twenty-eight-foot long countertop

made out of a single stainless steel pressing, complete with recessed sinks and draining surfaces. An equally generous feature is the open shelving above the countertop, backed by a band of continuous fenestration facing southeast.

One of the most exposed spaces of the cottage is the dining room, which not only opens directly onto the living space but also features a plate glass window with re-entrant corners overlooking the lake. The living room is handled as one large glazed partition where rounded glass corners serve to continue the hermetic feeling of the space. This organic sense of enclosure is further emphasized by an undulating timber ceiling that caps the double-height volume. The upper part of this space is pierced by a square clerestory, the glazing of which is screened by vertical timber louvers, inside and out.

Alternations in the basic floor finish pass from granite to oak, and vice-versa, and are continued throughout with similar connotations: granite is used for the more public areas, particularly in the family room at the lower level. The room opens out onto the original rockface of the site. An atypical element at this level is the internal stair linking the ground and lower ground floors and inflecting inward for the last five threads. This organic gesture seems to have been introduced to accommodate additional storage against the northeastern retaining wall of the lower floor. The swerving of the stair afforded the architects an occasion to showcase a theatrical treatment of the timber balustrading.

The more one contemplates the horizontal thrust of the cottage with its crowning form jutting out toward the lake, the more one is reminded of the horizontal emphasis of Wright's Prairie Style, particularly as this manifested itself most decisively in his Robie House, Chicago, of 1909. At Point William we have much the same formal stress on the main living floor, reinforced in this instance by sharp steel cornices overhanging the northeastern and southwestern elevations. This profile continues around the head of the building, culminating in an extra-deep cornice extending from the face of the kitchen in order to cover the barbeque and counter serving the main deck.

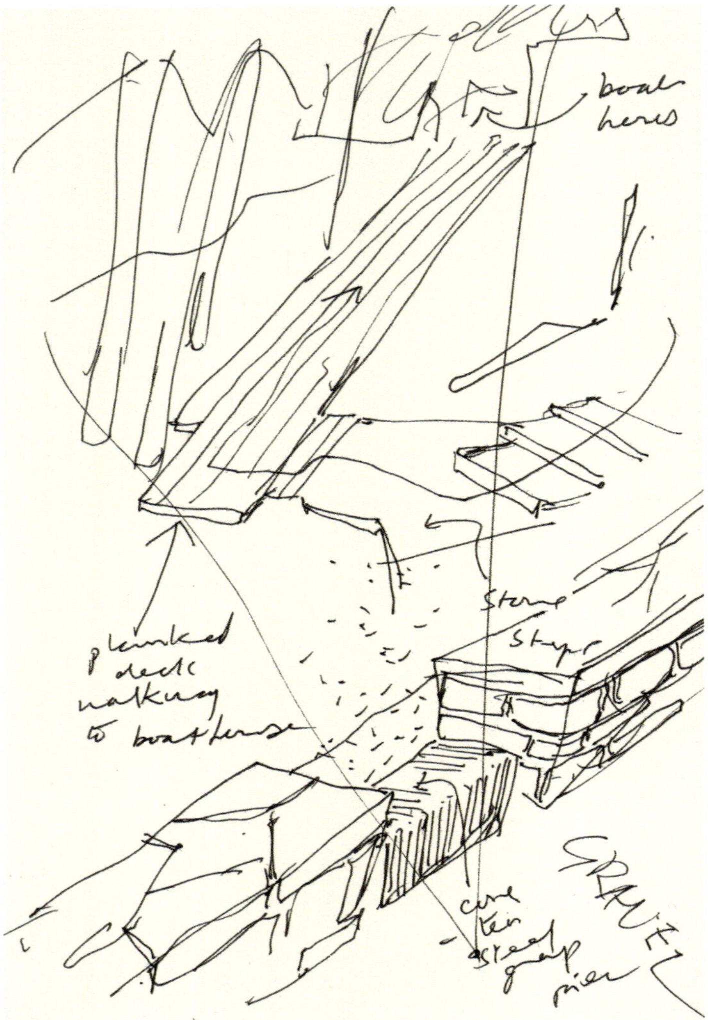


The southwestern elevation is clearly the back of the building, and here again one senses an echo of the utilitarian rear of the Robie House. Apart from a single, free-standing steel stair with timber treads that descends from the deck to the rockface, the southwestern elevation of the cottage underemphasizes features of architectural interest. Of significance here is the contrast between the field stone walls that enclose the undercroft, the lack of openings on its northeastern face, and its amply fenestrated southwestern face, which not only provides recessed picture windows lined with steel plate for each of the bedrooms on the lower ground floor, but also a large picture window with plate glass doors linking the lower family room with the primordial rockface.

From a tectonic standpoint, the cottage is a hybrid structure with reinforced concrete playing an important initial role in the grounding of the building on this rugged and difficult site. This is never more evident than in the concrete retaining wall, which is faced in field stone throughout the undercroft. Of equal consequence are the reinforced concrete slabs underpinning the ground floor that also serve to establish the lower level against the rock. Reinforced concrete is equally present in the blade walls and columns that carry the concrete slab of the ground floor. However, the essential structure is variously made up of steel stanchions, timber framing, and rafters that support the roof and culminate in the undulating ceiling of the double-height living volume that opens out toward the lake in two directions. In this regard, the double and single free-standing concrete columns within the dining area solely serve as symbolic articulations of the space, since they evidently carry no load once they are above the ground floor. However, they do indeed support the slab above the lower ground floor.

With the singular exception of the cottage, a reflected ceiling plan is the crucial tectonic principle throughout the site. However, there is a gradual shift in the relative expressivity of the soffit as one passes from the elaborate articulation of the underside of the roof in the boathouse to the total revetment of the framing in the cottage. There, with the exception of the concrete structure, the framing has been finished in Douglas fir, either in the form of plywood linings and fittings, or as a boarded ceiling over the foyer where the wide planks with inset light fittings alternate with narrow battens to create a syncopated pattern across the length of the soffit. At the same time, with this singular work, Shim-Sutcliffe have taken their talent for precision cabinetwork to new levels of refinement. Moreover, they have entered fully into the challenge of creating a total work of art that is particularly evident in the specially designed hardware light fittings and one-off furniture pieces.

Like Aalto's Villa Mairea, completed on the Aalstrom family's Noormarku Estate in 1939, the cottage at Point William is a "head" building in that the pivoting thrust of its main living volume juts out toward the expanse of the lake. It is a dynamic climax to the movement of the entire compound as it projects its crystalline picture-windowed volumes off the singular rock that obtrudes onto the site at this point, as if it were the concentrated embodiment of the genus loci. To this end, the fine-grained, dark-gray granite surface of the commanding serpentine walkway, edged in weathering steel, makes its final undulations before the foyer of the house, almost as if it is genuflecting to the imperious mass of the intervening rock. Simultaneously, the "head" of the cottage pivots in two directions, first toward the immovable rock and the rest of the compound, and second toward the infinite expanse of the lake.

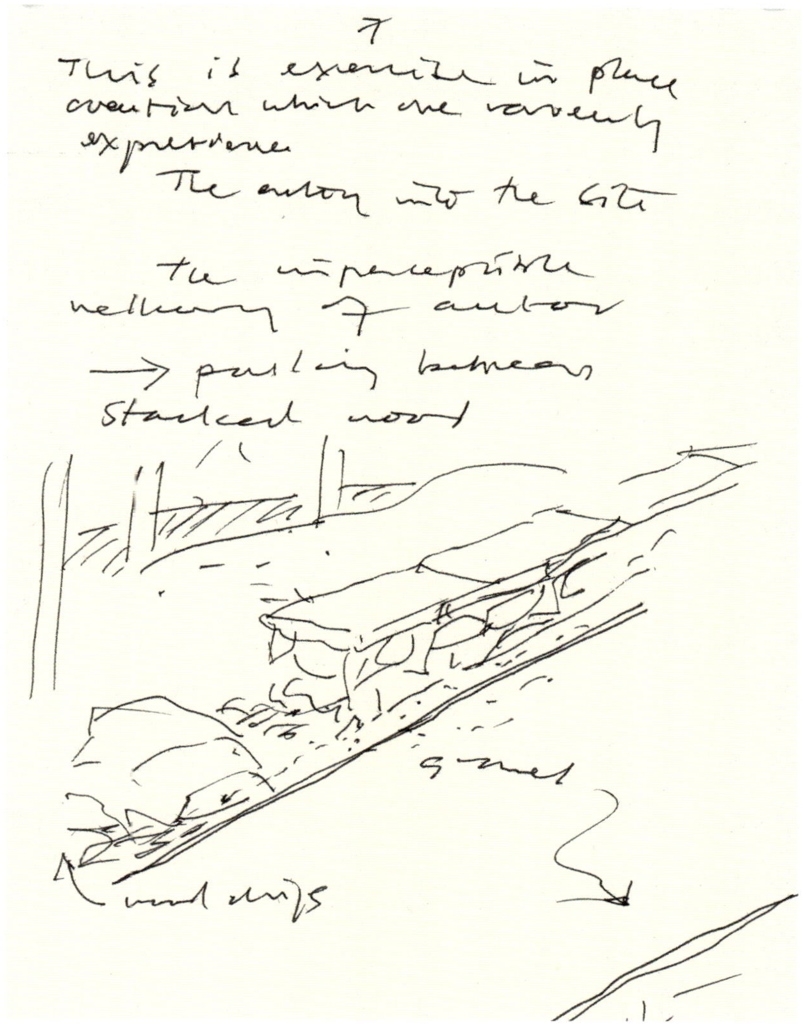

In the last analysis, one becomes imperceptibly aware that the ground itself is a layered work, a sensuous palimpsest to be read as much by the entire corporal being as much as by the eyes. There is the subtle significance of the woodchips underfoot that are as olfactory as they are tactile. The fine-grained, granite gravel is held in position like an improbable carpet by invisible stainless steel anchors. And although it is unexpectedly elevated in the boathouse, the dyadic, natural/artificial cultivation of moss lying underfoot is a microscopic rain forest that unfolds like a creviced, bottomless micro-escarpment around the perimeter of the guest cottage. Perennially hovering above the site, the moss possesses an ambiguous, oneiric character in that it never touches down, much like the battened timber walkways across the telluric, stereotomic site, a site that barely tolerates vegetation on the face of its geological otherness. For this is the Canadian Shield in all its enigmatic glory, tolerating the roots of conifers that inescapably perpetrate its cracks as it rolls into the silent profundity of the infinite, mist-covered lake system that attends Point William on every side. ▪

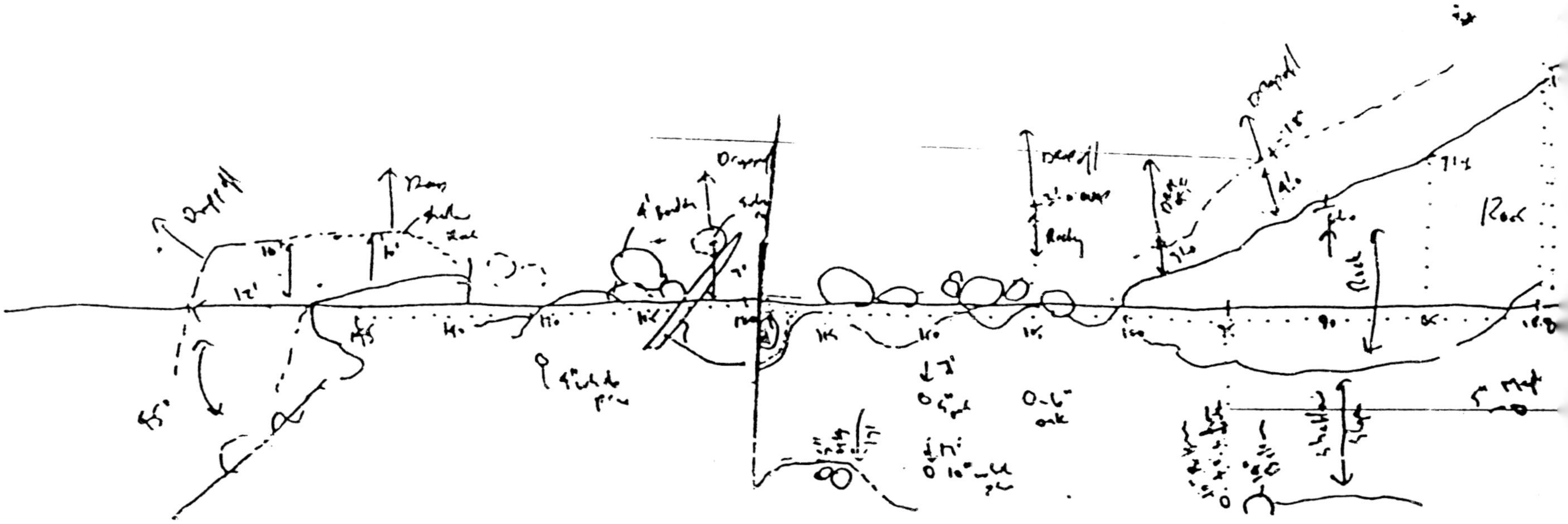

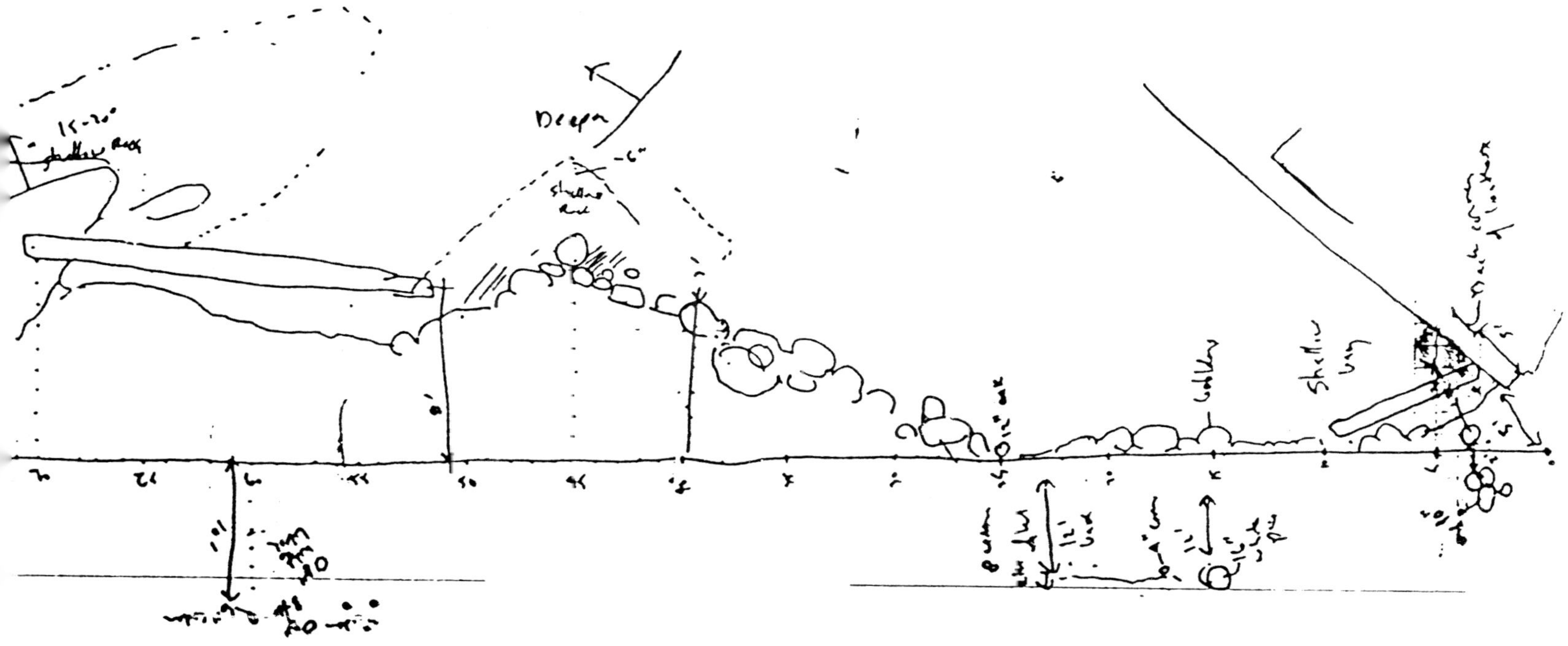

# The Boathouse

1997-1999

The first built work at Point William, the boathouse accommodates two interior boat slips and one exterior slip at the lake level, and sleeping accommodation above. Two boats enter parallel to the shoreline allowing the facade facing out to the lake to represent the constructional strategies for the building. The exterior boat slip enters perpendicular to the shoreline and engages with a wooden dock. Heavy timber walls extend upward from the robust wood cribbing that forms the foundations and protects the finer woodwork of the inner layer.

oct 96 Shell Boathouse

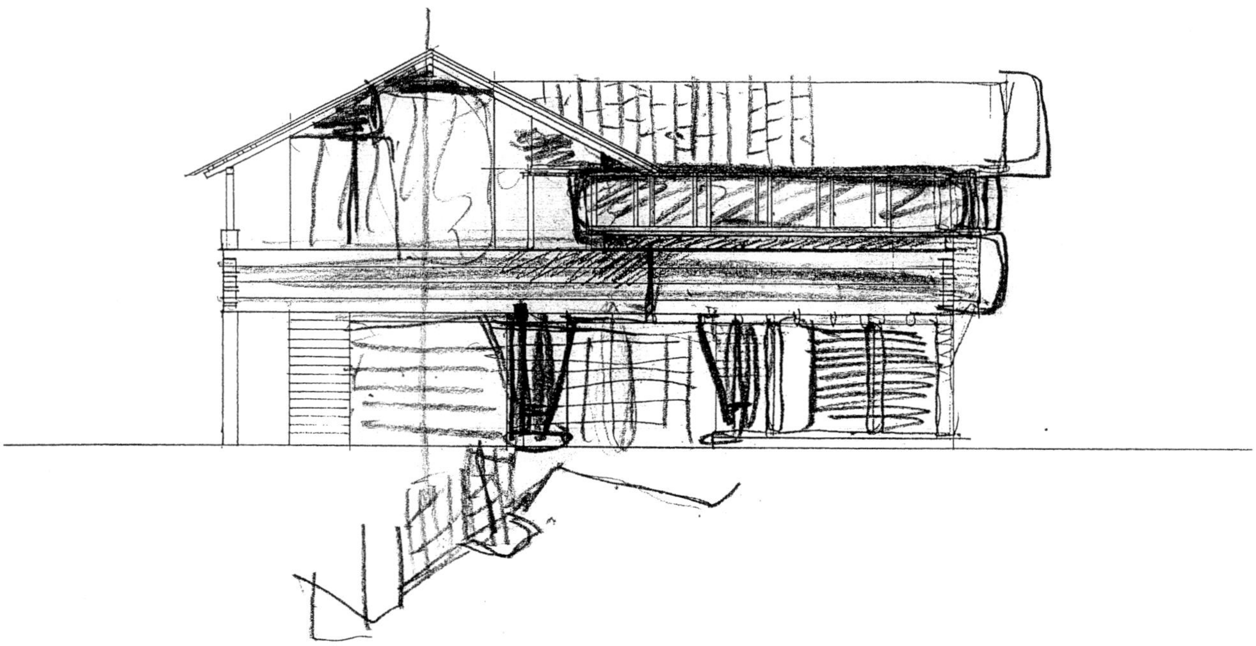

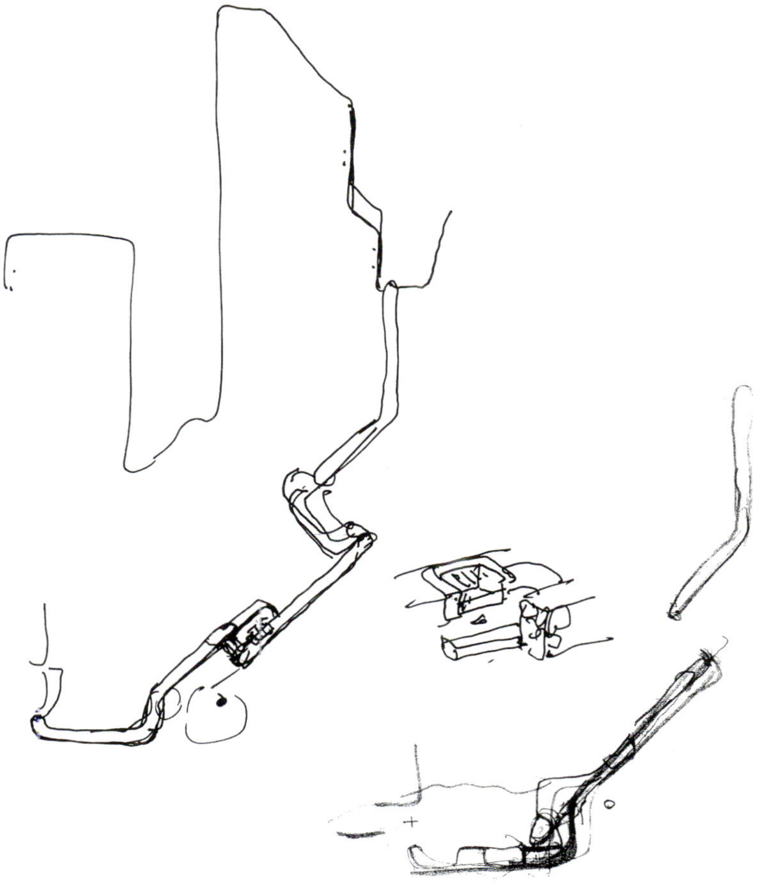

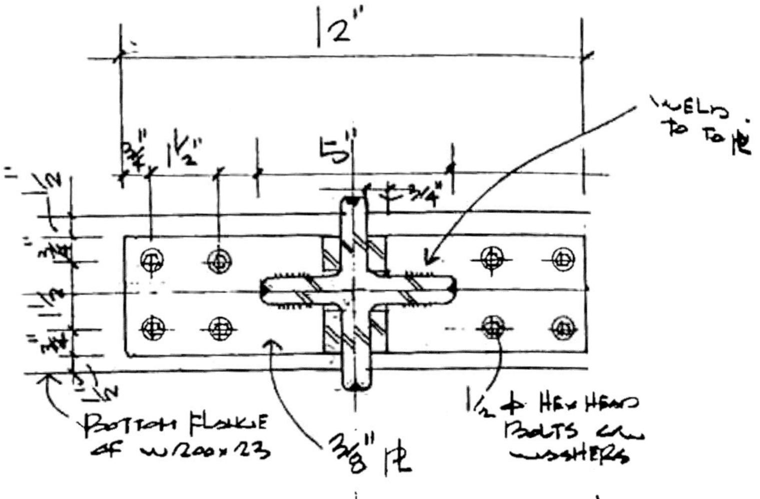


REFLECTED PLAN @ 'CAPITOL'
3" = 1'-0"

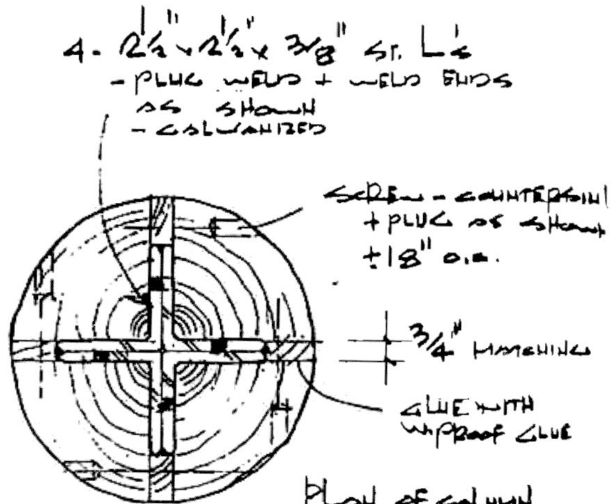


PLAN OF COLUMN
3" = 1'-0"

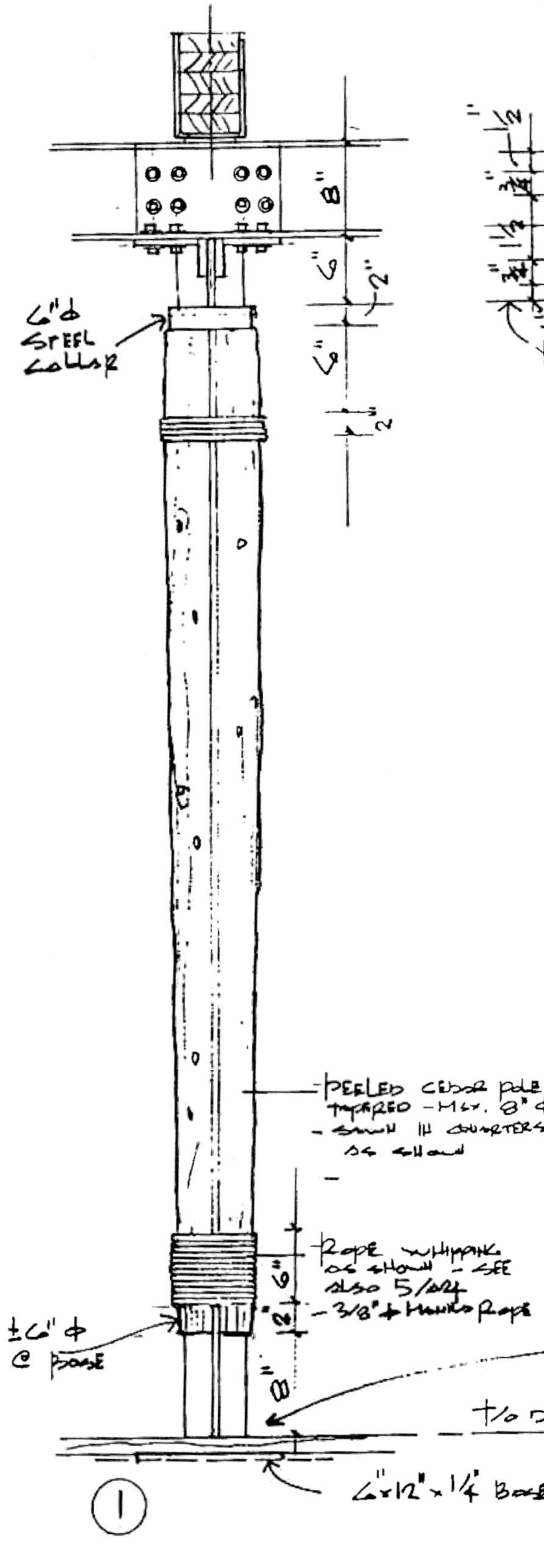

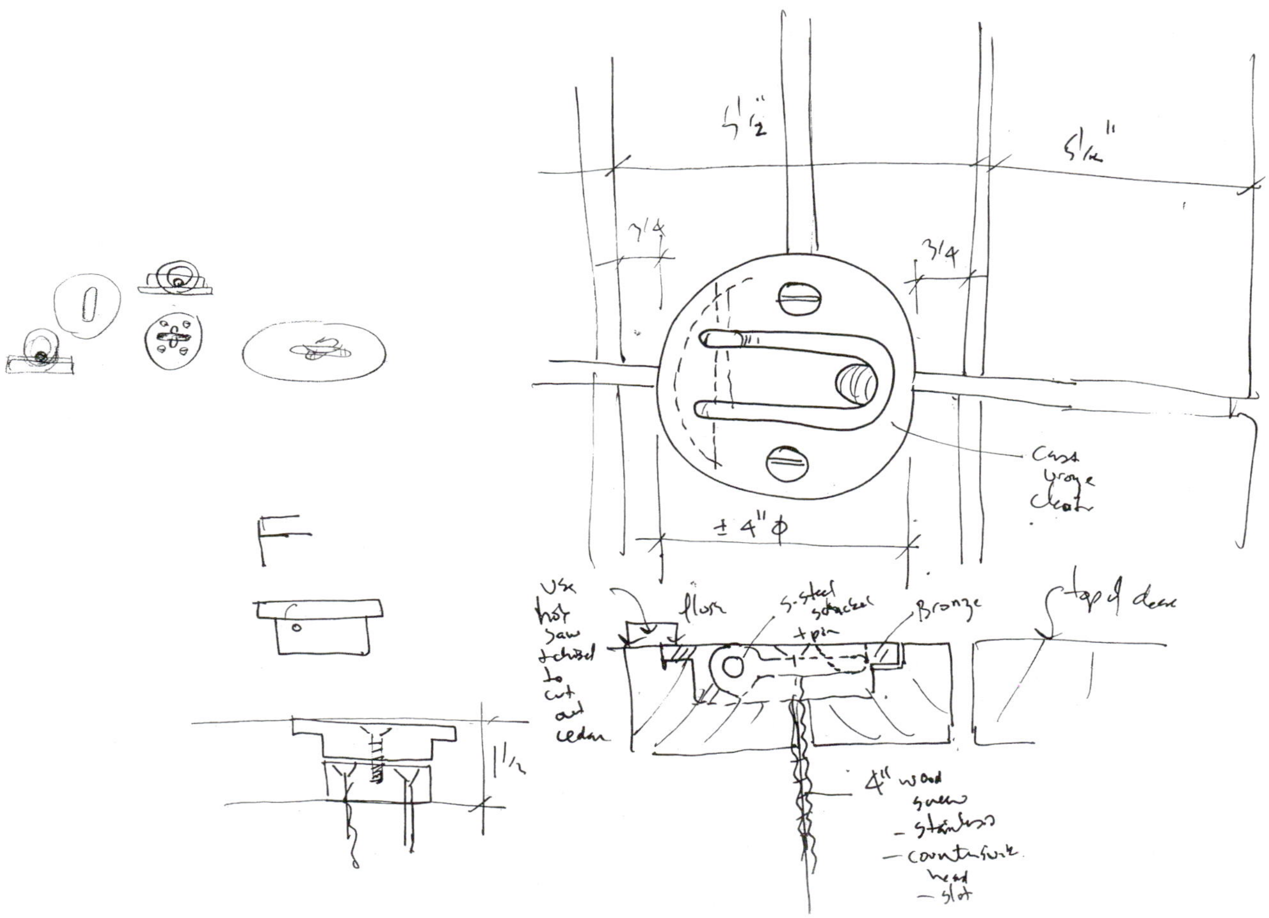
5 1/2"
5 1/4"
3/4
3/4
Cast bronze cleat
± 4" Φ
Use hot saw & chisel to cut out cedar
flush
s-steel shackle + pin
Bronze
top of deck
1 1/2
4" wood screw
– stainless
– countersunk head
– slot

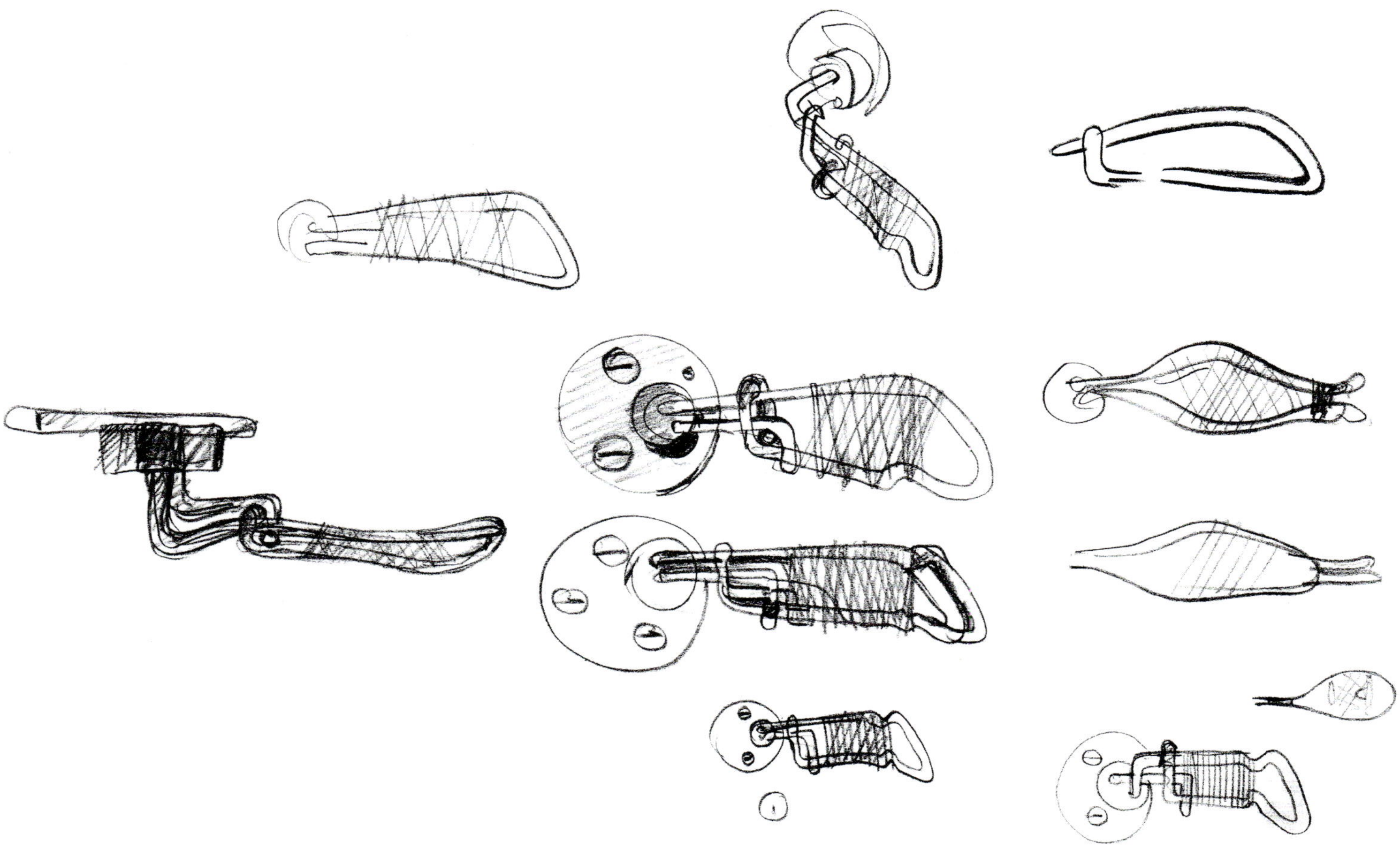

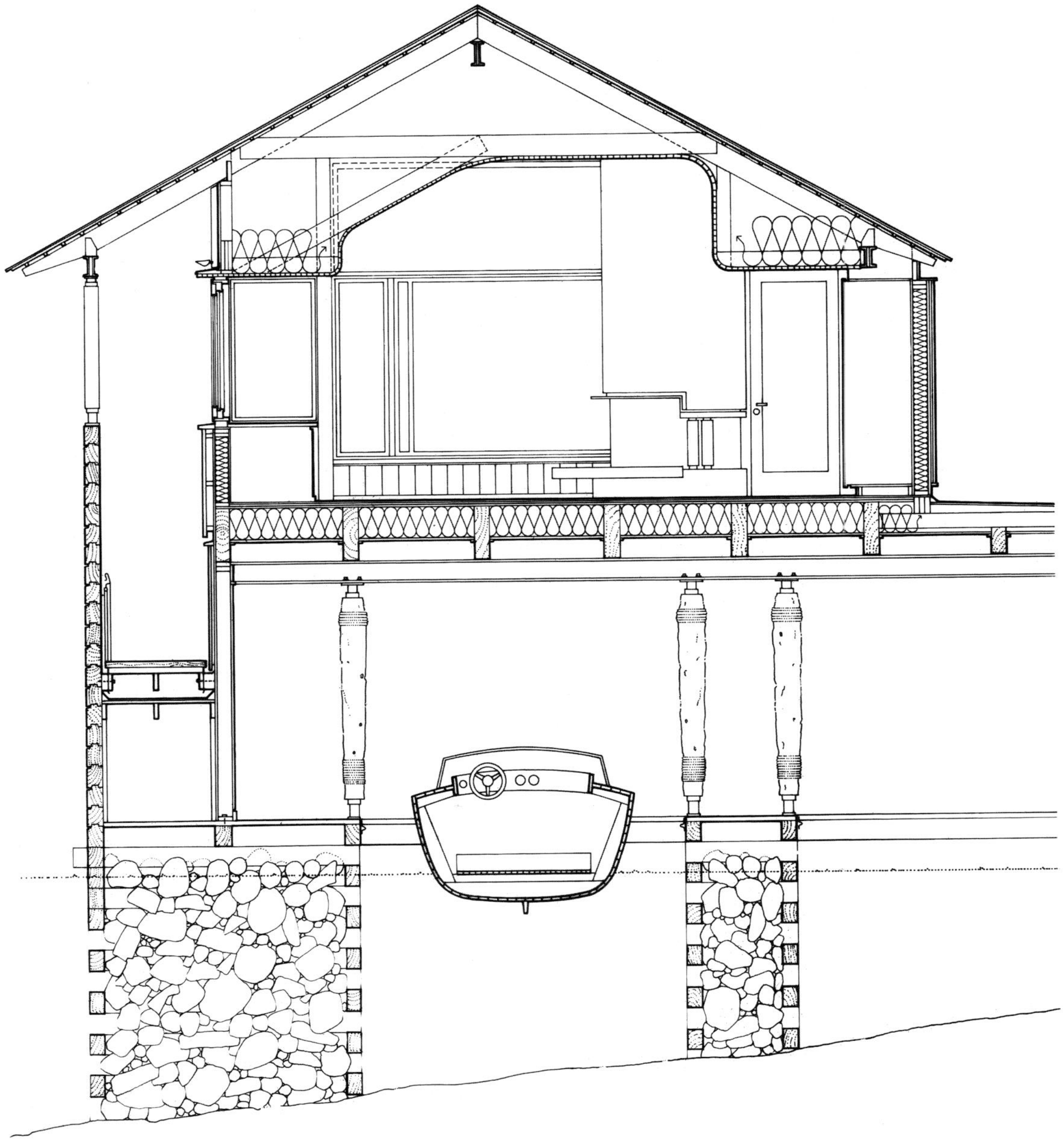

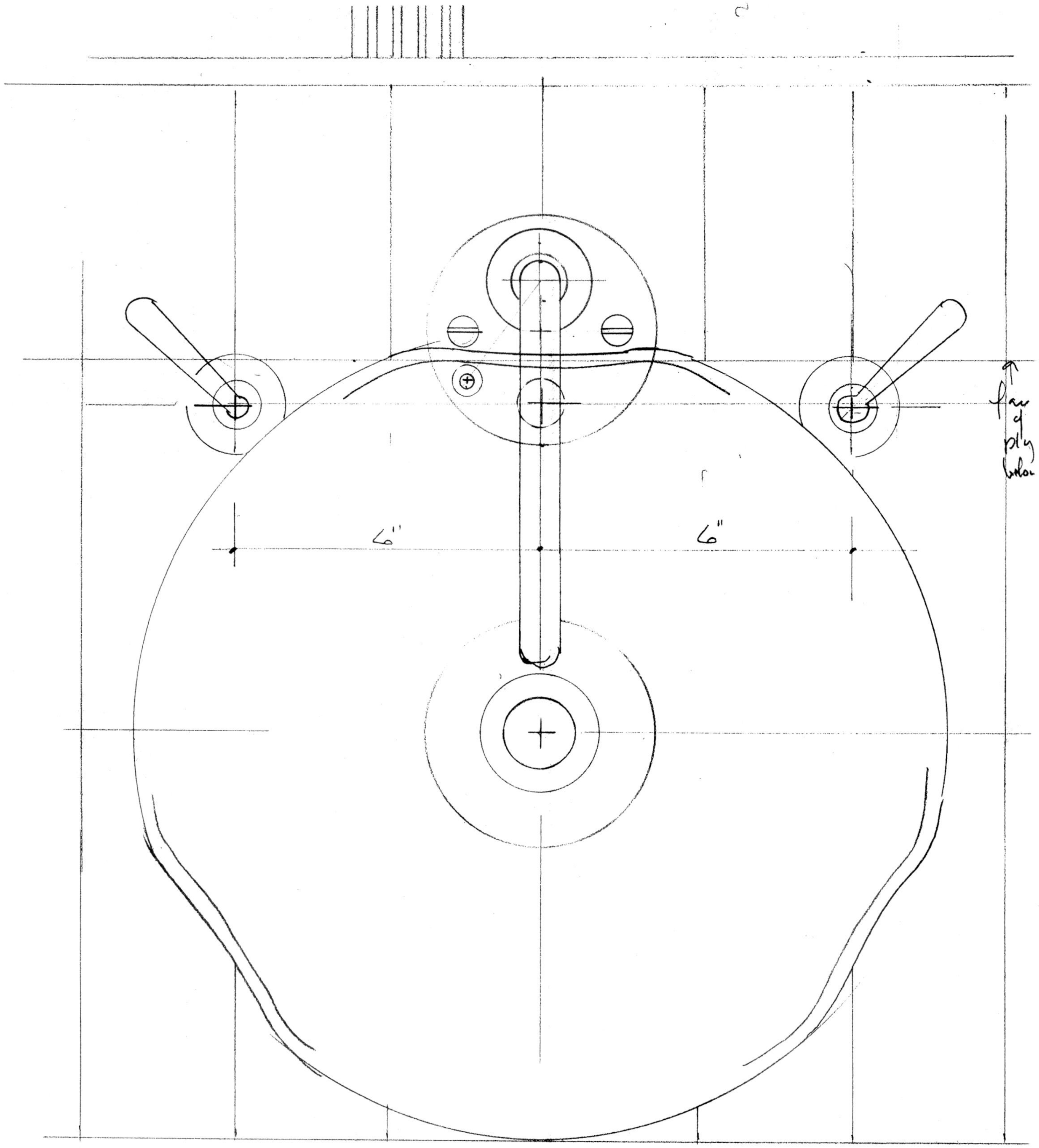
6"
6"
face of ply below

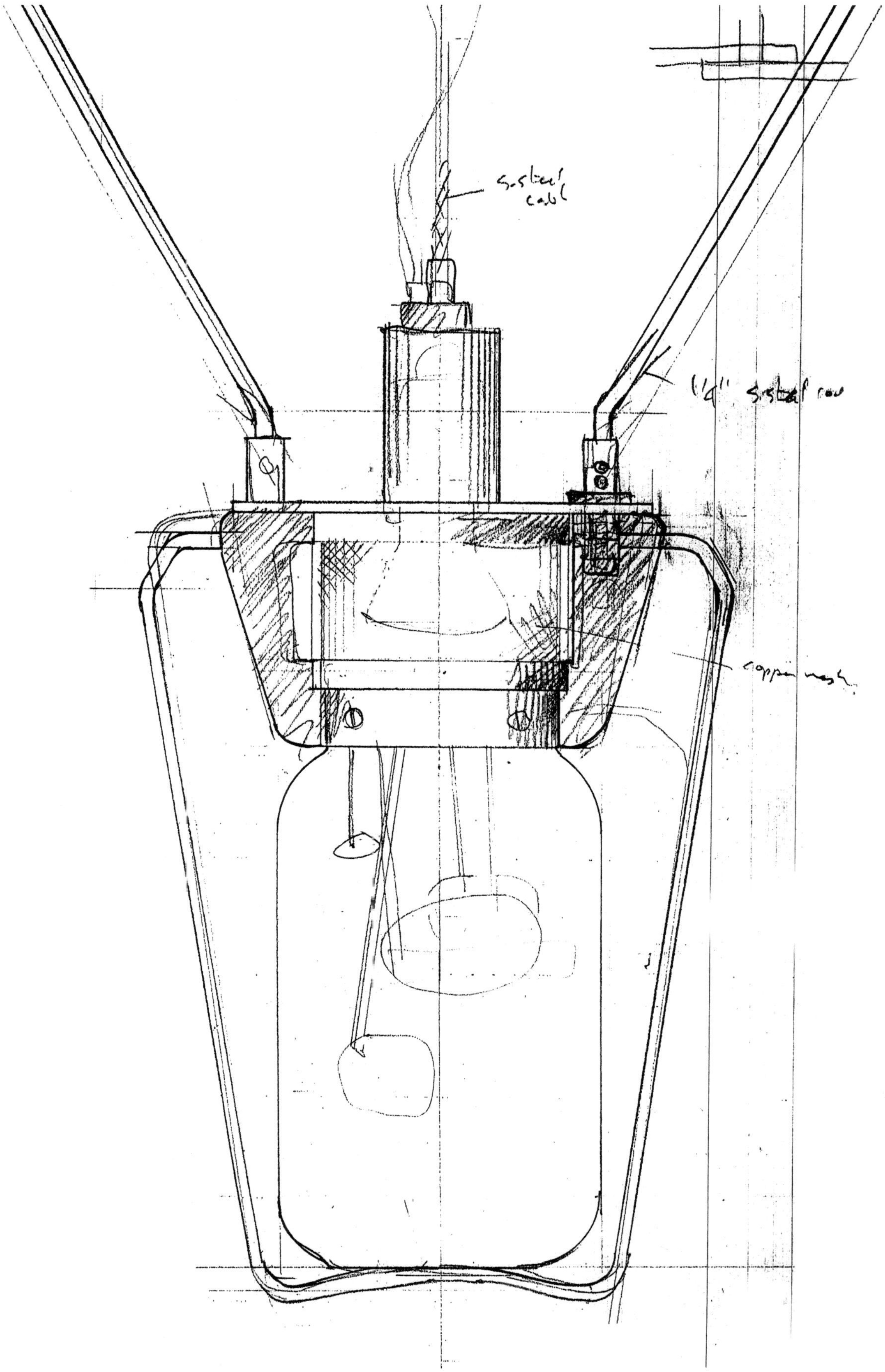
s.steel cable
1/4" s.steel rod
copper mesh

# The Guest Cottage

2007-2010

*View of original cabin built at the turn of the century.*

The second building at Point William reconstructs the pre-existing 1910 vernacular cabin with its central core and wraparound porch. These distinct spaces are clearly articulated by both circulation and material palette. The floor, walls, and ceiling of the inner core are lined in Douglas fir wood. The porch spaces inside and out are made legible through the use of exposed wood decking ceilings and stacked firewood exterior walls. Weathering steel is used to clad the building's roof and horizontal siding creating a rich textural reading.

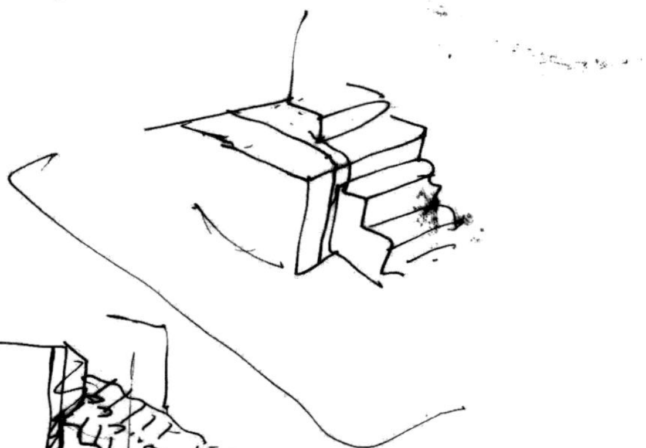

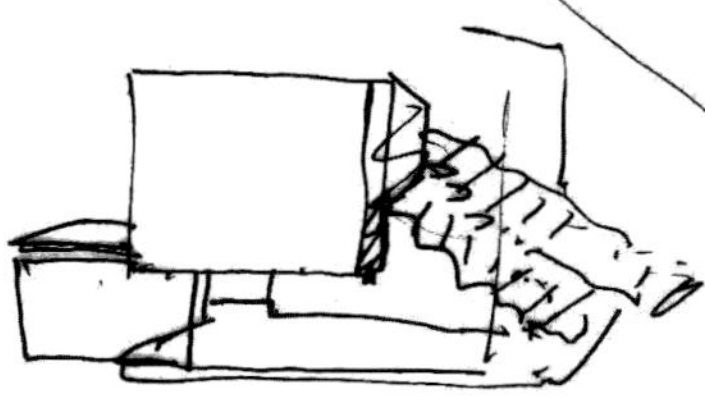

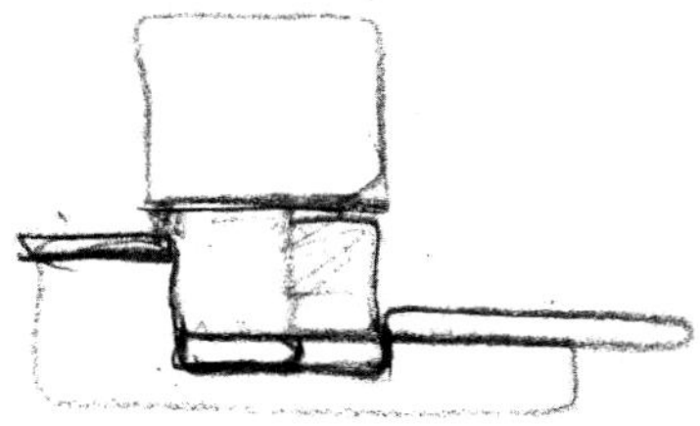

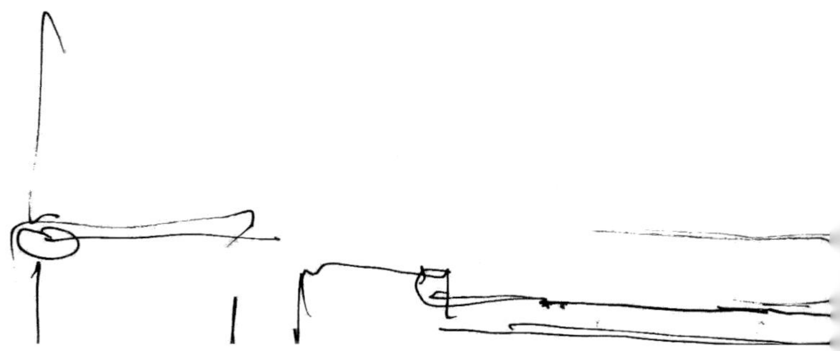

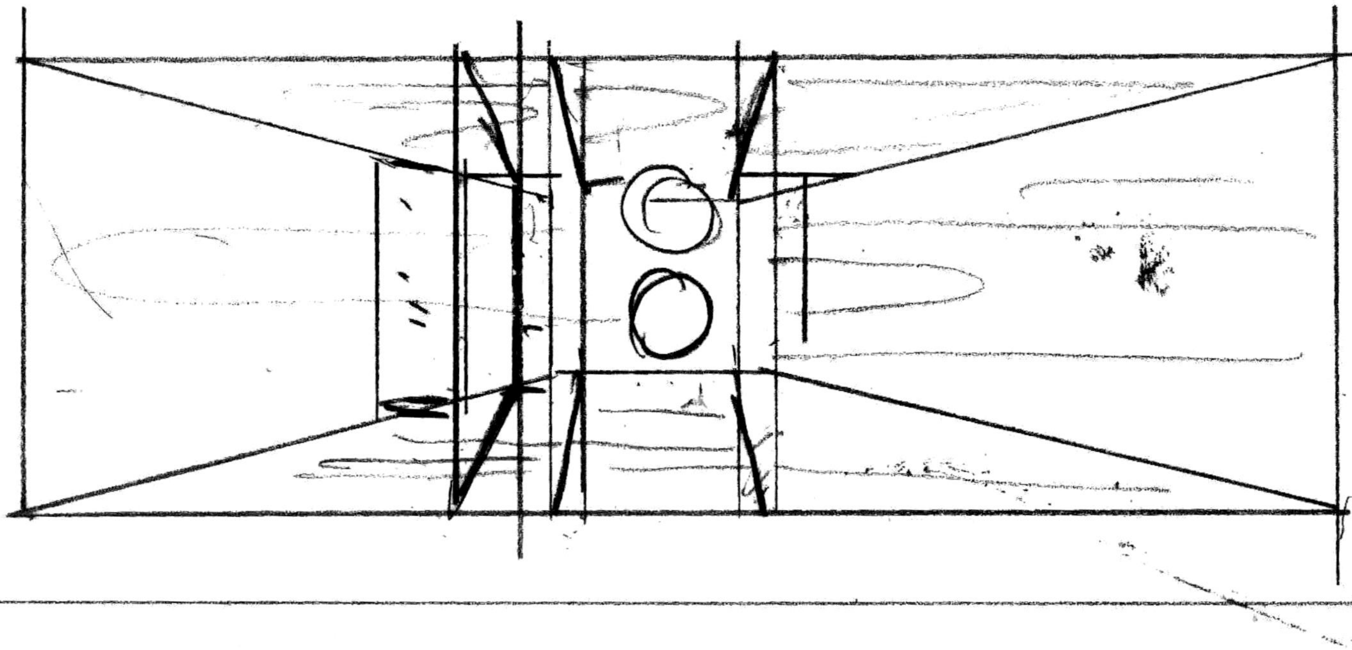

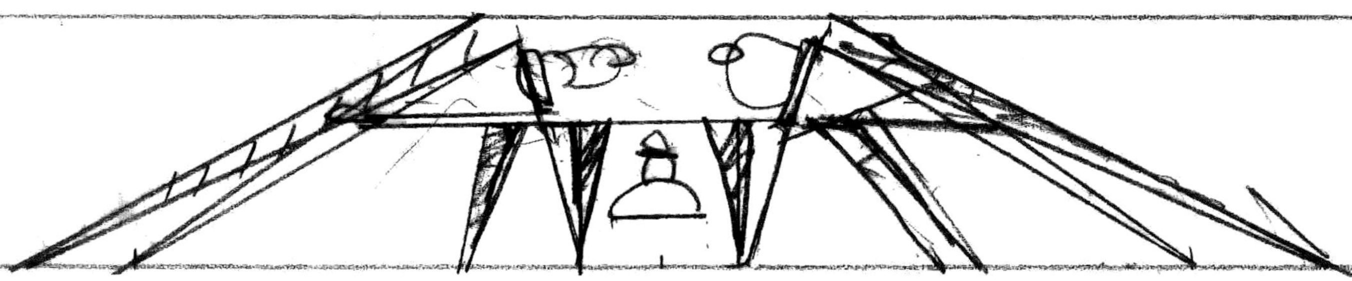

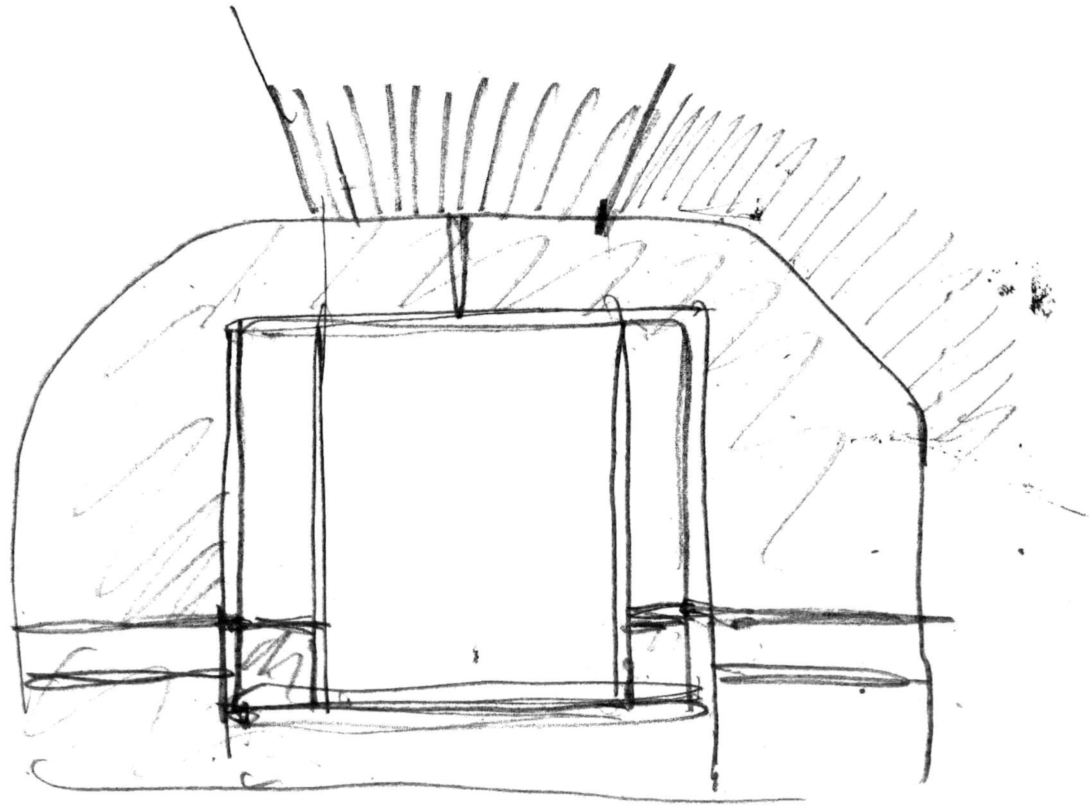

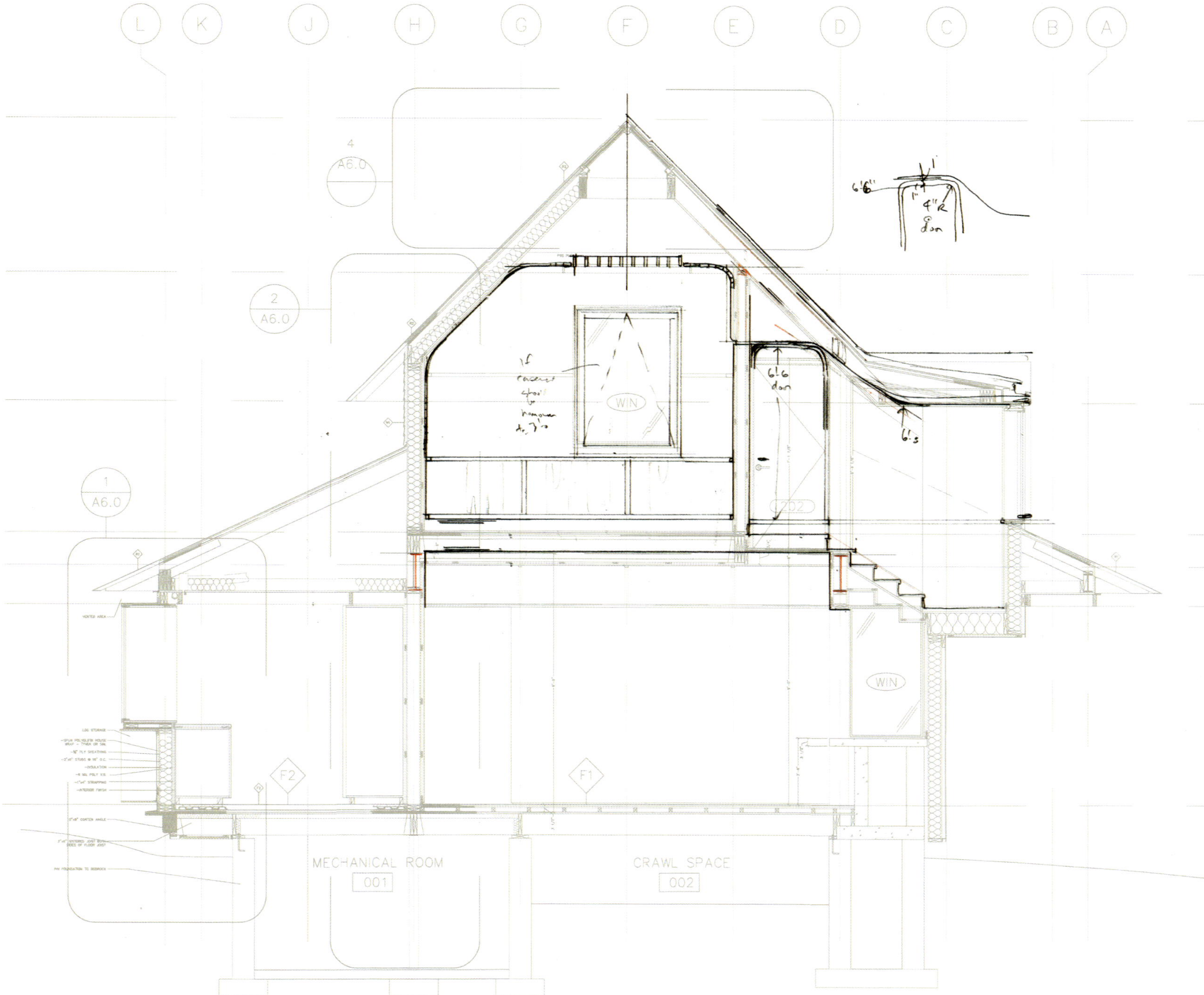

L
K
J
H
G
F
E
D
C
B
A
4
A6.0
2
A6.0
1
A6.0
WIN
WIN
F2
F1
MECHANICAL ROOM
001
CRAWL SPACE
002

# The Cottage

2010-2017

Point William's architectural promenade weaves its way from forest to clearing and through the cottage to the water's edge. The new residence partially uses the footprint of the existing cottage from the 1960s and also erases portions to reveal a large, granite outcropping, which now defines both the site and the cottage. Inside the cottage, deep weathering steel fins create cinematic spaces revealing the Canadian Shield landscape beyond. The articulated sections create both intimate and dramatic spaces that lead you to the water's edge.

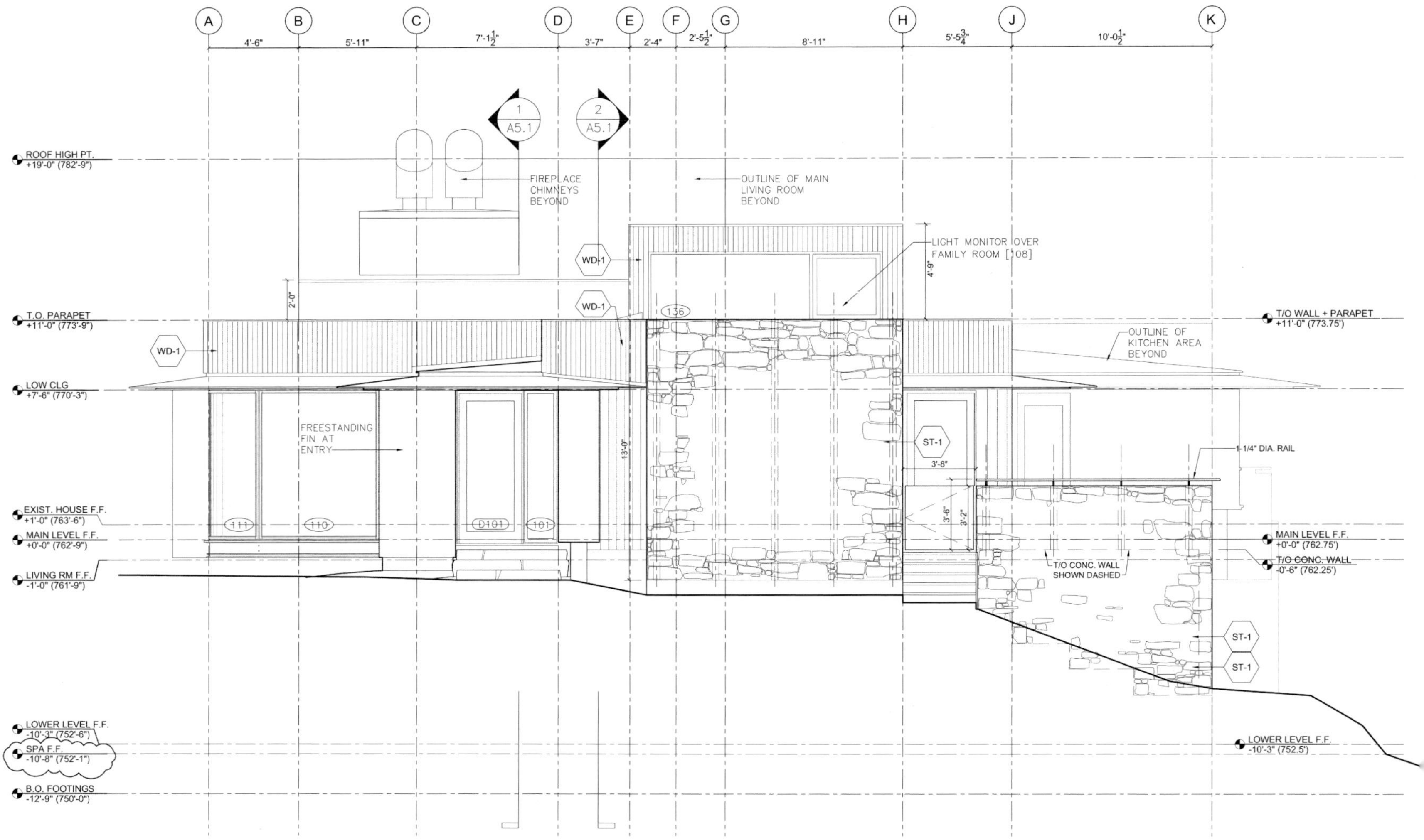

A
B
C
D
E
F
G
H
J
K
4'-6"
5'-11"
3'-7"
2'-4"
8'-11"
1
A5.1
2
A5.1
ROOF HIGH PT.
+19'-0" (782'-9")
FIREPLACE
CHIMNEYS
BEYOND
OUTLINE OF MAIN
LIVING ROOM
BEYOND
LIGHT MONITOR OVER
FAMILY ROOM [108]
WD-1
T.O. PARAPET
+11'-0" (773'-9")
T/O WALL + PARAPET
+11'-0" (773.75')
OUTLINE OF
KITCHEN AREA
BEYOND
LOW CLG
+7'-6" (770'-3")
FREESTANDING
FIN AT
ENTRY
ST-1
1-1/4" DIA. RAIL
EXIST. HOUSE F.F.
+1'-0" (763'-6")
MAIN LEVEL F.F.
+0'-0" (762'-9")
MAIN LEVEL F.F.
+0'-0" (762.75')
T/O CONC. WALL
-0'-6" (762.25')
T/O CONC. WALL
SHOWN DASHED
LIVING RM F.F.
-1'-0" (761'-9")
LOWER LEVEL F.F.
-10'-3" (752'-6")
SPA F.F.
-10'-8" (752'-1")
LOWER LEVEL F.F.
-10'-3" (752.5')
B.O. FOOTINGS
-12'-9" (750'-0")

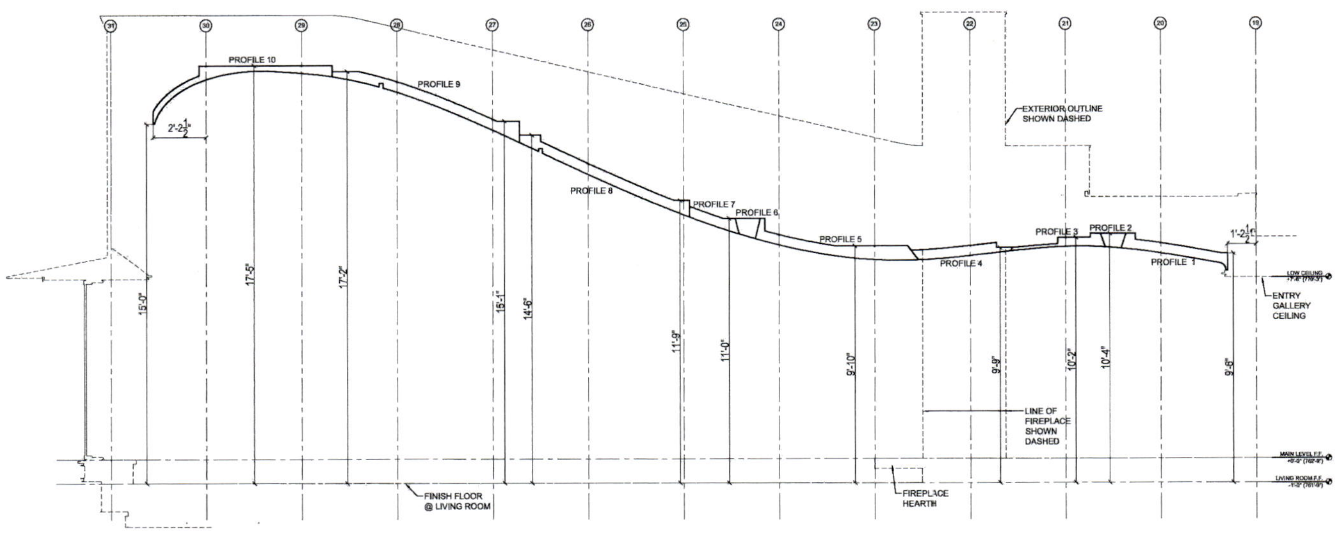


*Above: Section through sub-framing for living room ceiling.*

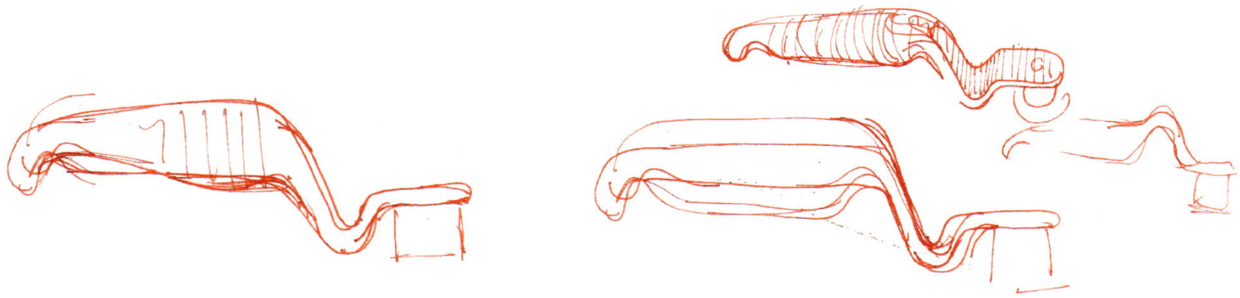

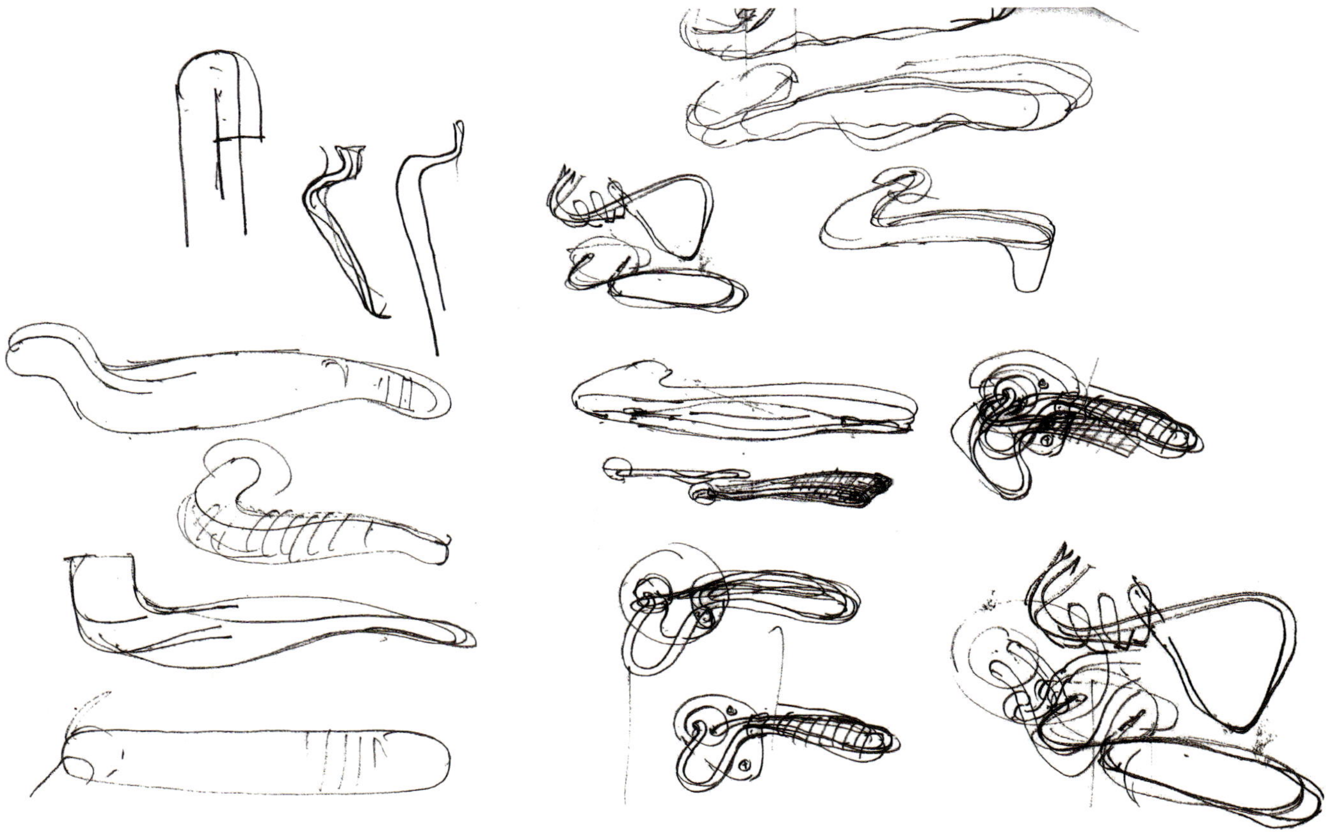

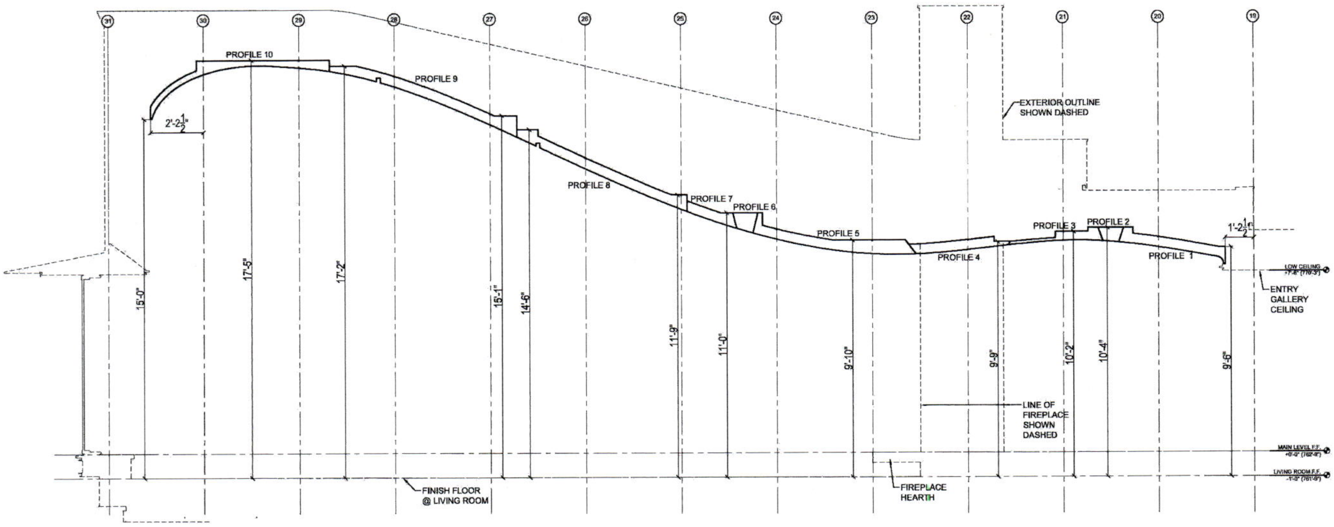


Above: Section through sub-framing for living room ceiling.

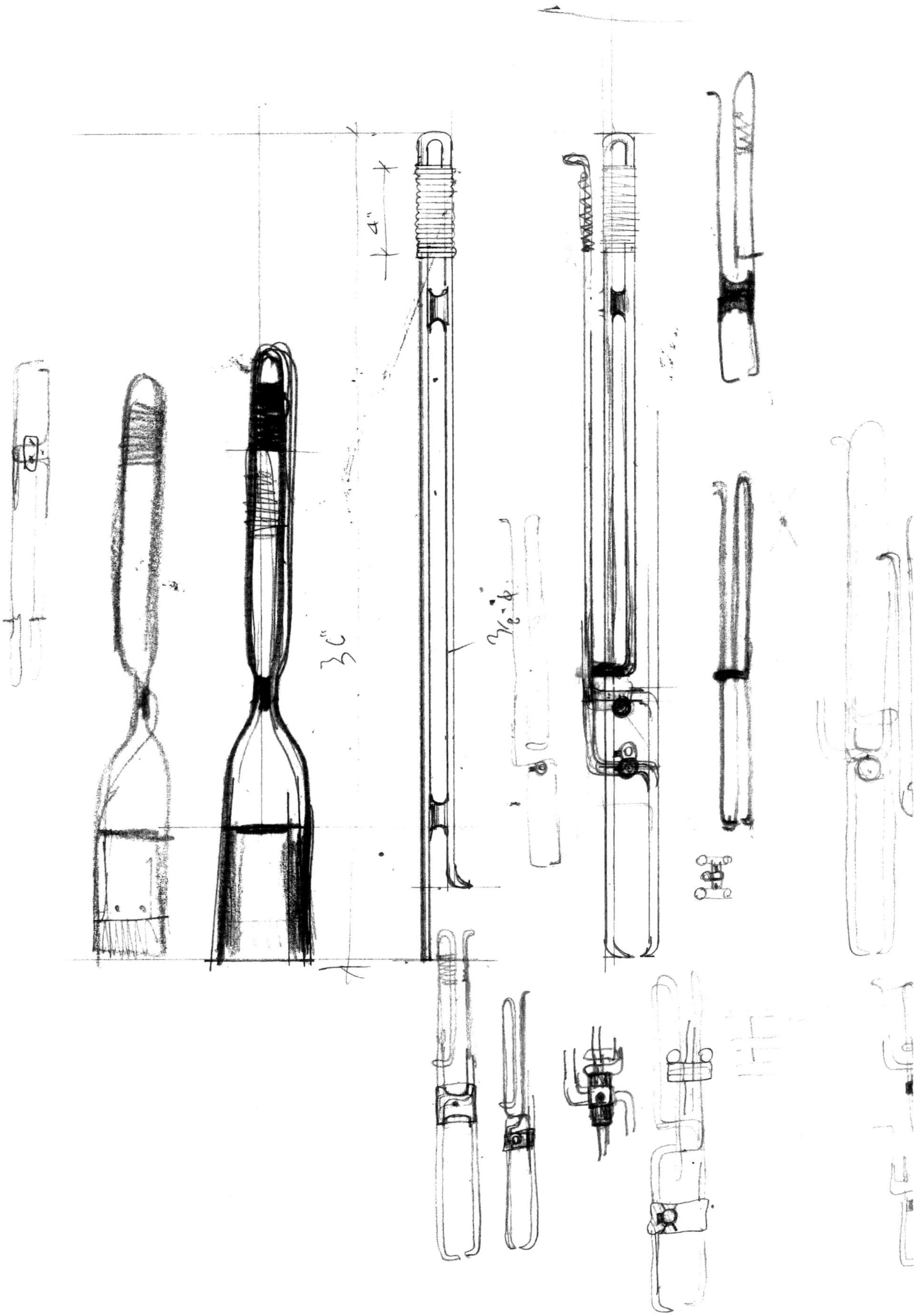

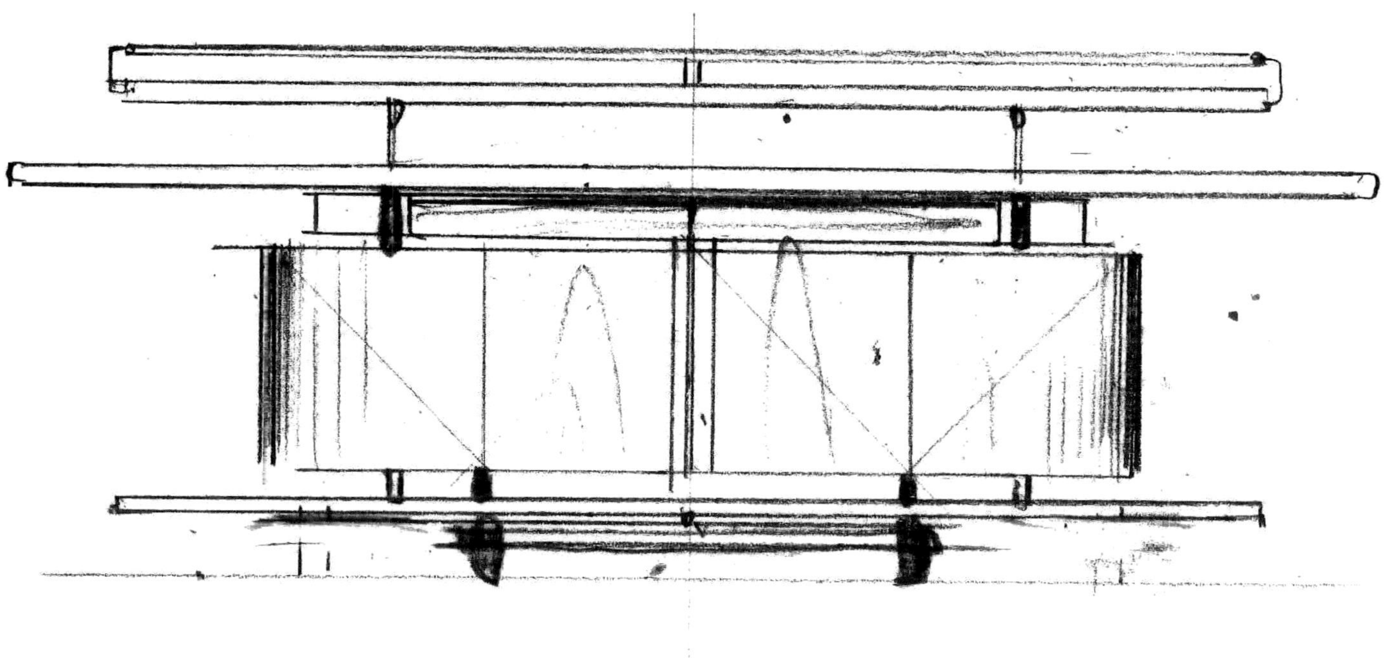

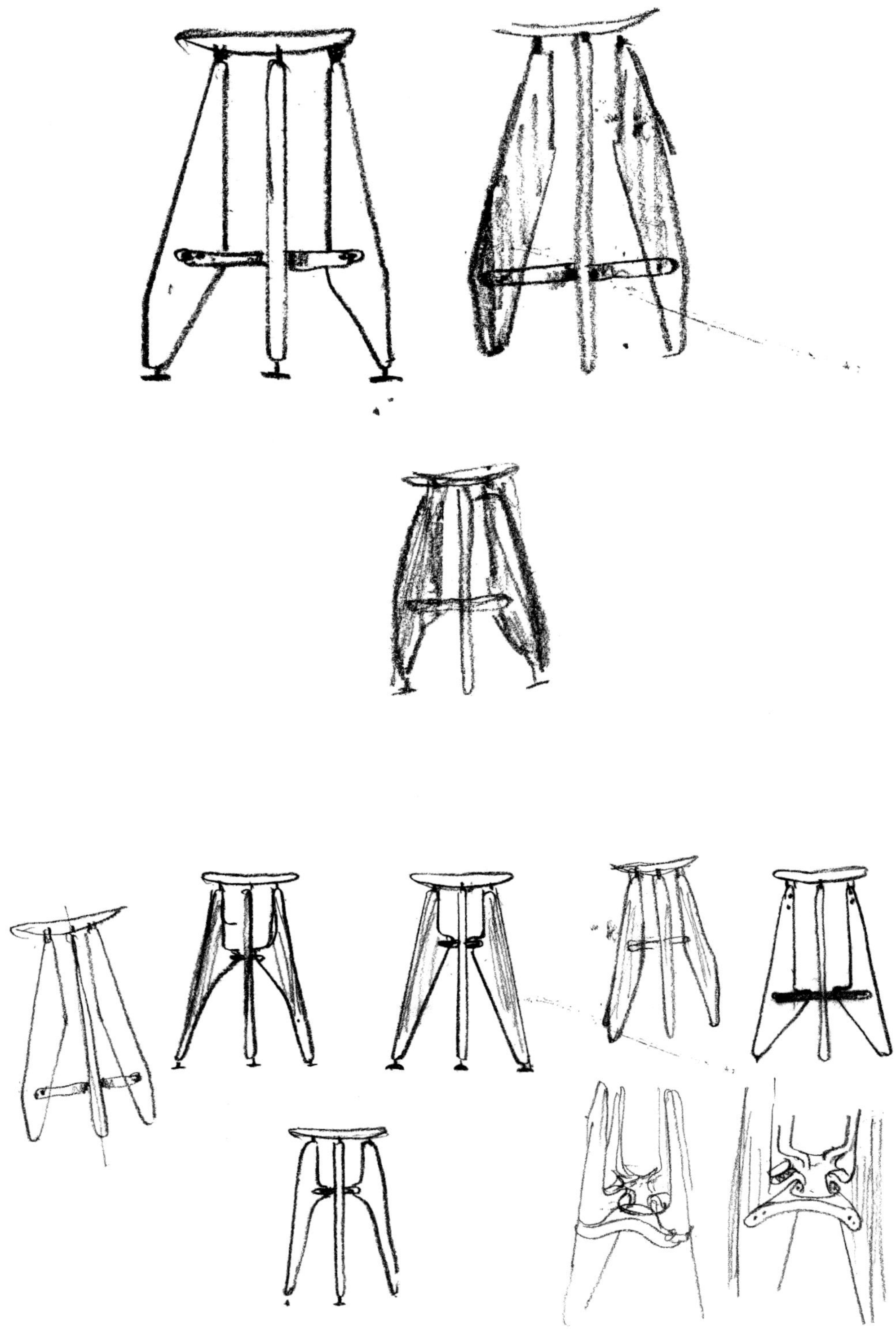

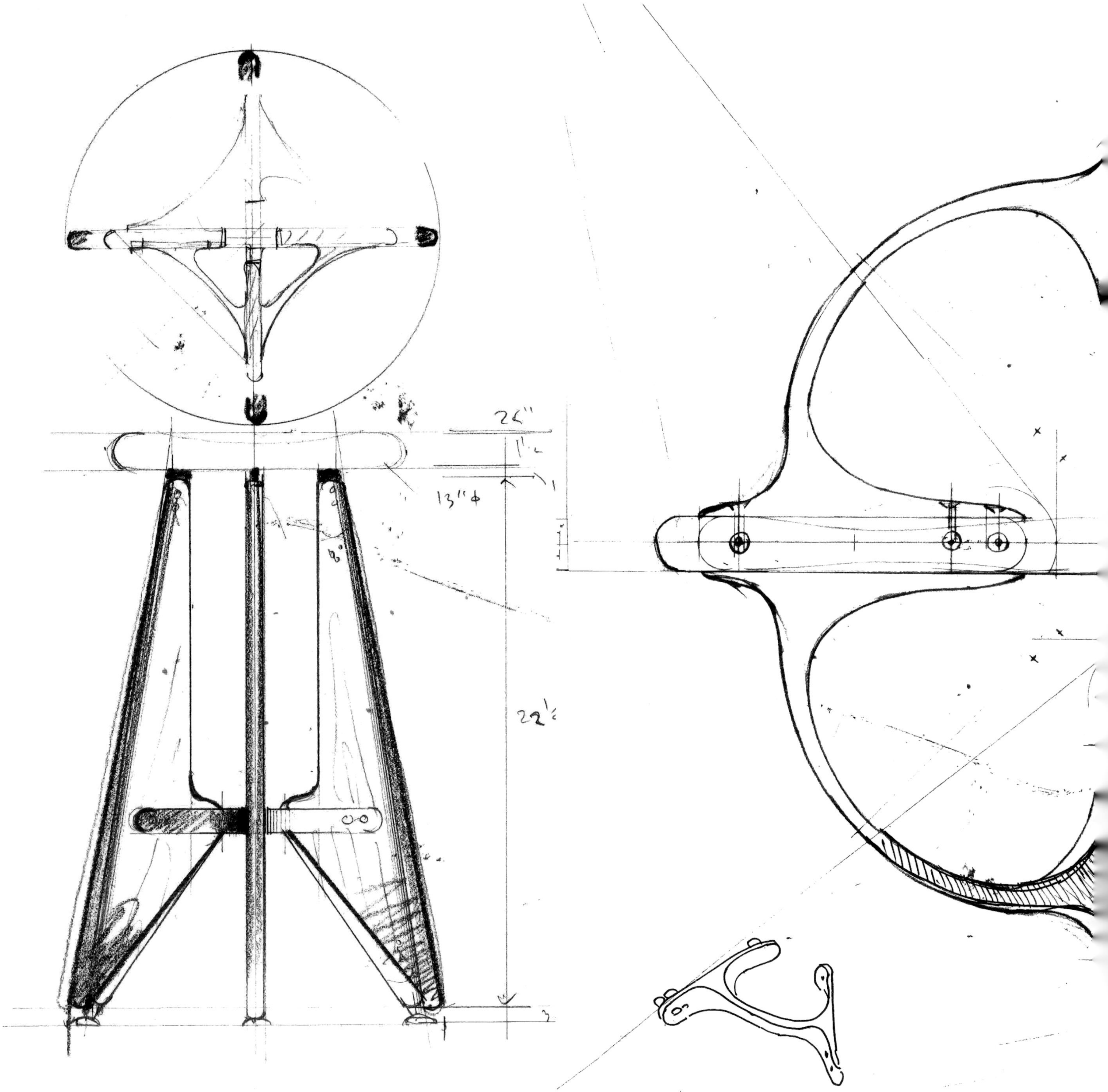

26"
13"ϕ
22½

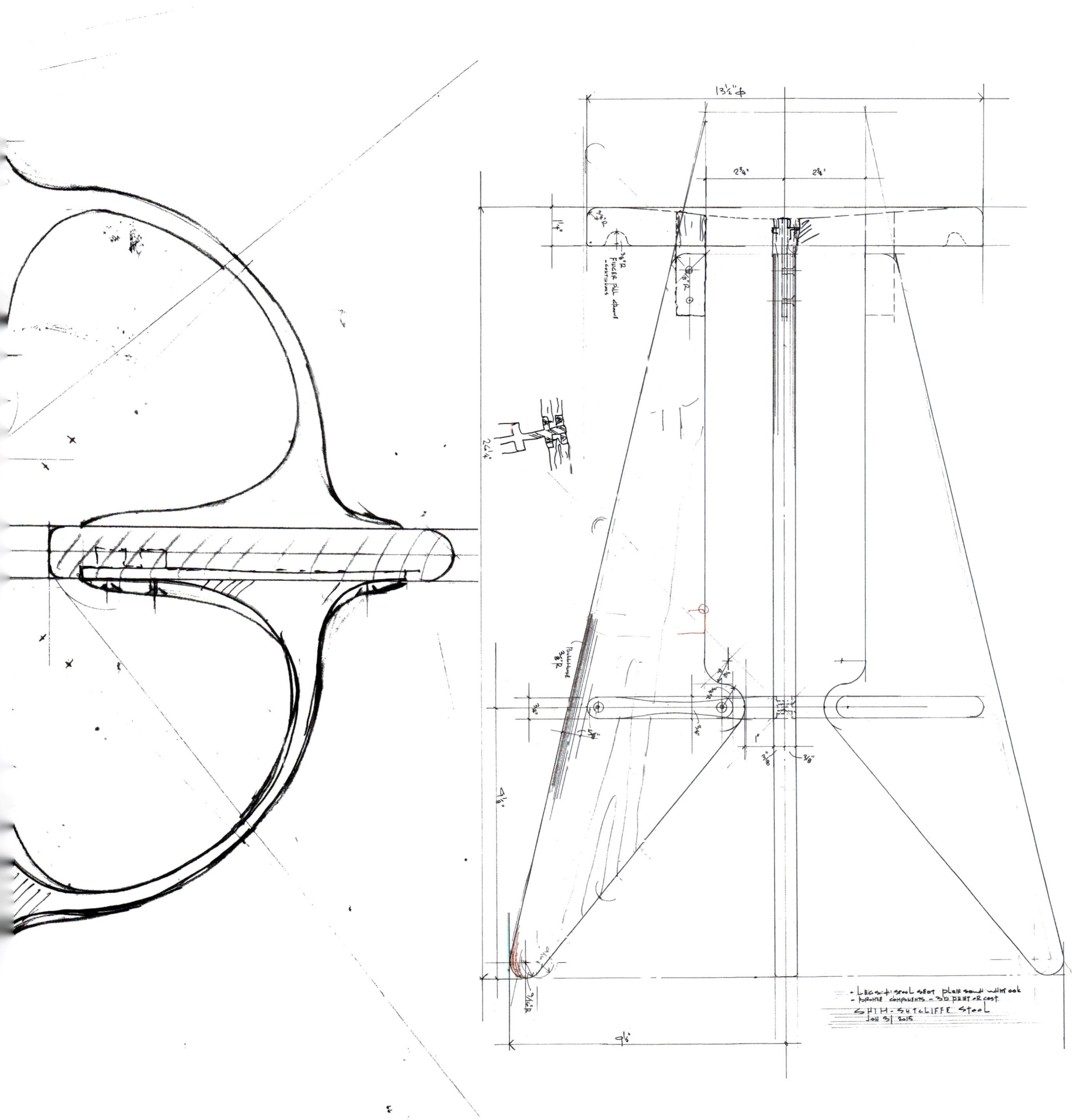
- BRONZE COMPONENTS - 3D PRINT OR CAST.
SHIH-SUTCLIFFE STOOL

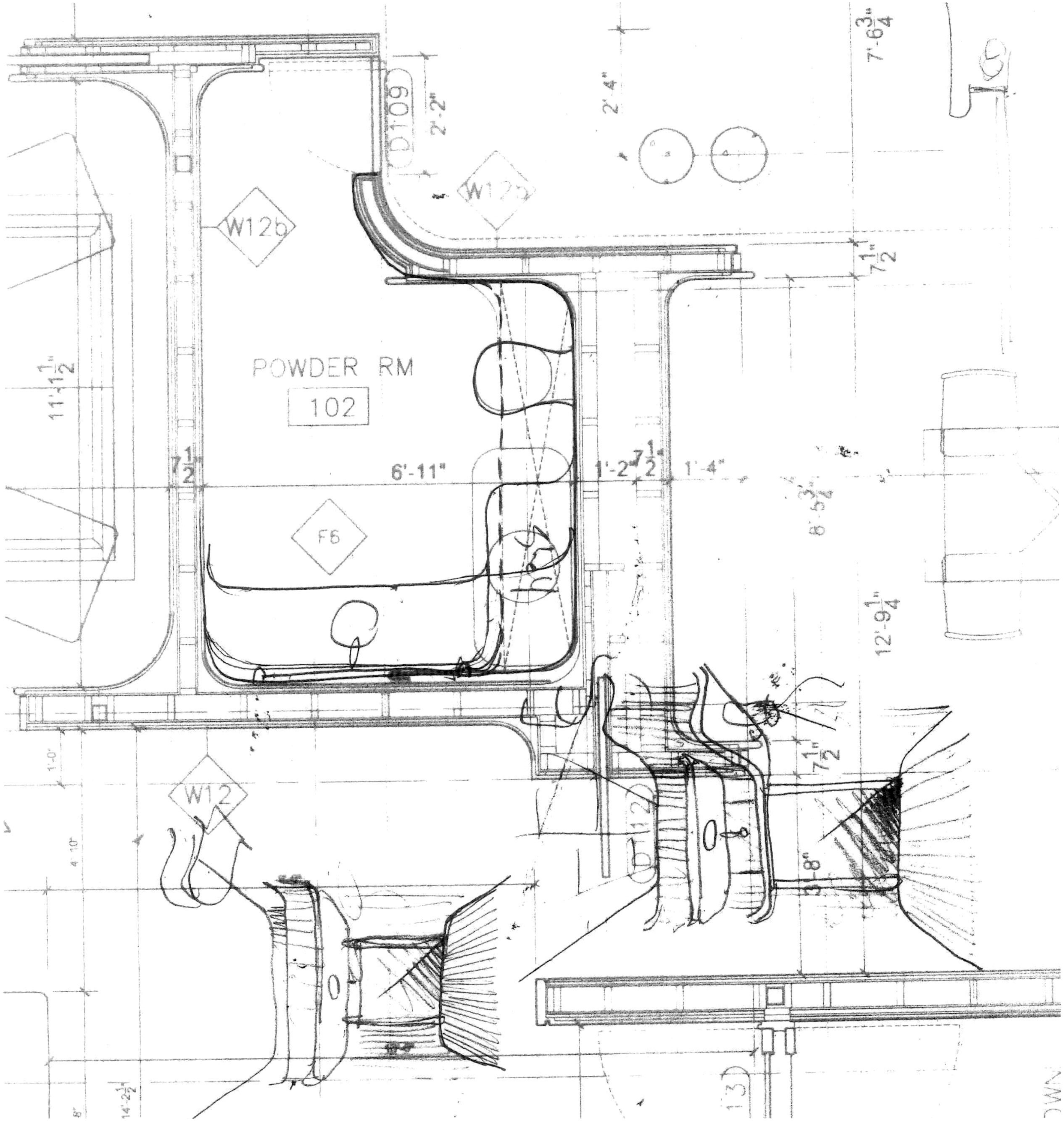
POWDER RM
102
6'-11"
F6
W12b
W12
D109
D112
2'-2"
2'-4"
1'-4"
7'-6 3/4"
12'-9 1/4"
11'-11 1/2"

RED NOTICE
BILL BROWDER
HERMIONE LEE
PENELOPE FITZGERALD
JONAS SALK
CAMPFIRE
collection

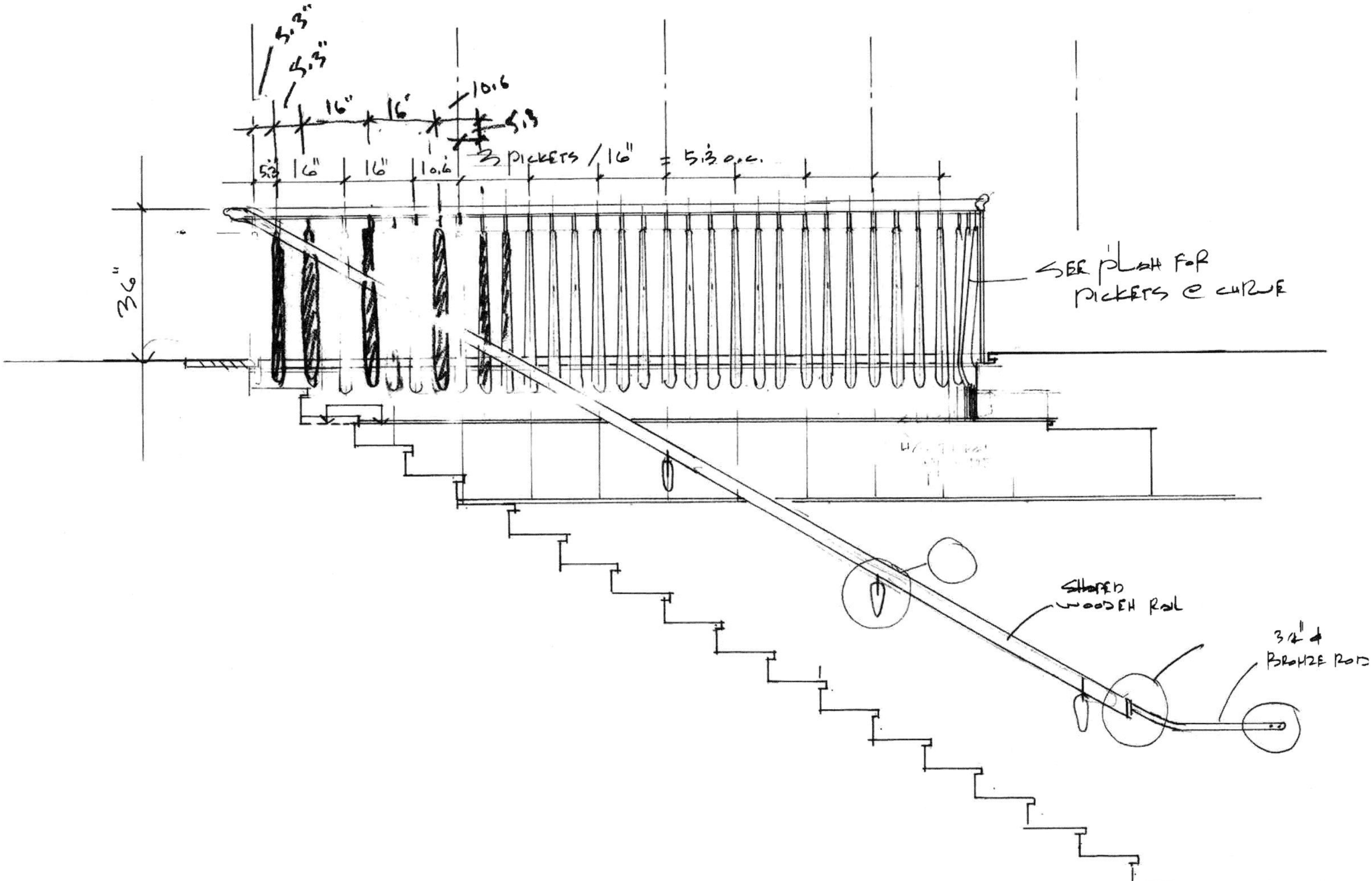


INTERIOR STAIR - PICKET
1/2" = 1'-0"

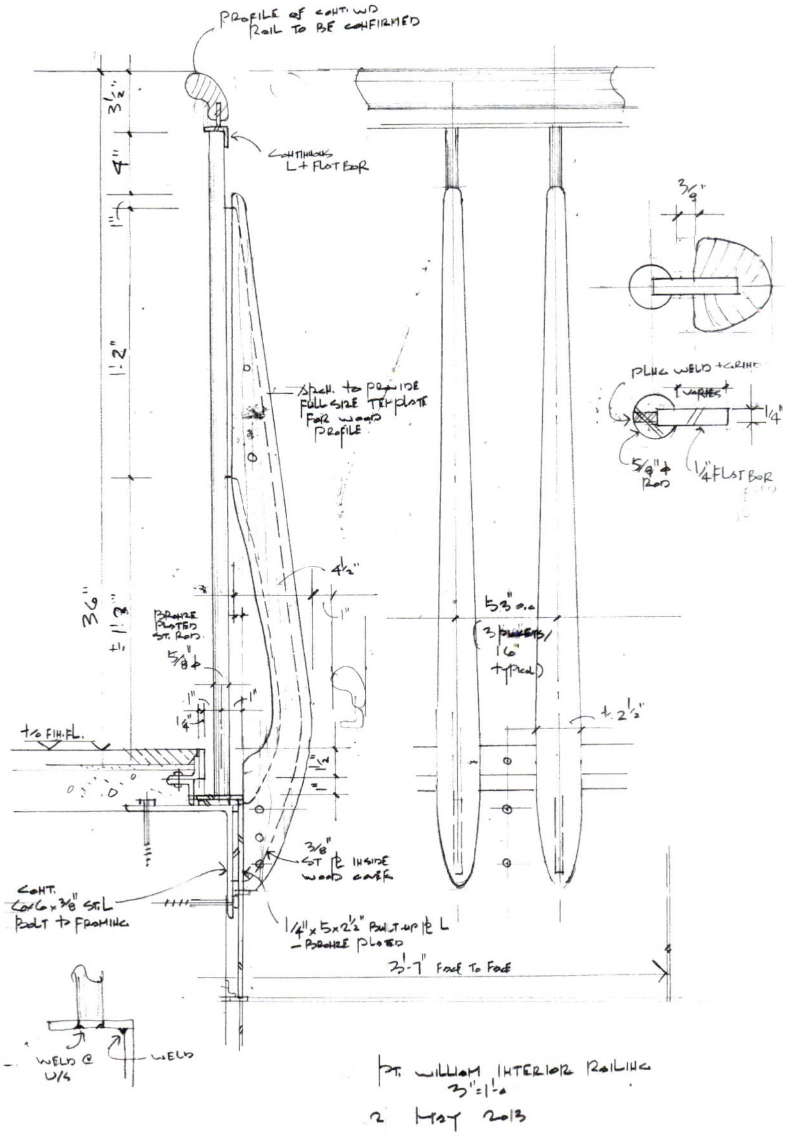
PROFILE of CONT. WD RAIL TO BE CONFIRMED
CONTINUOUS L + FLAT BAR
PLUG WELD + GRIND
1/4" FLAT BAR
3/8" ST PL INSIDE WOOD CASE
3'-7" FACE To FACE
WELD
PT. WILLIAM INTERIOR RAILING
3"=1'-0"
2 MAY 2013

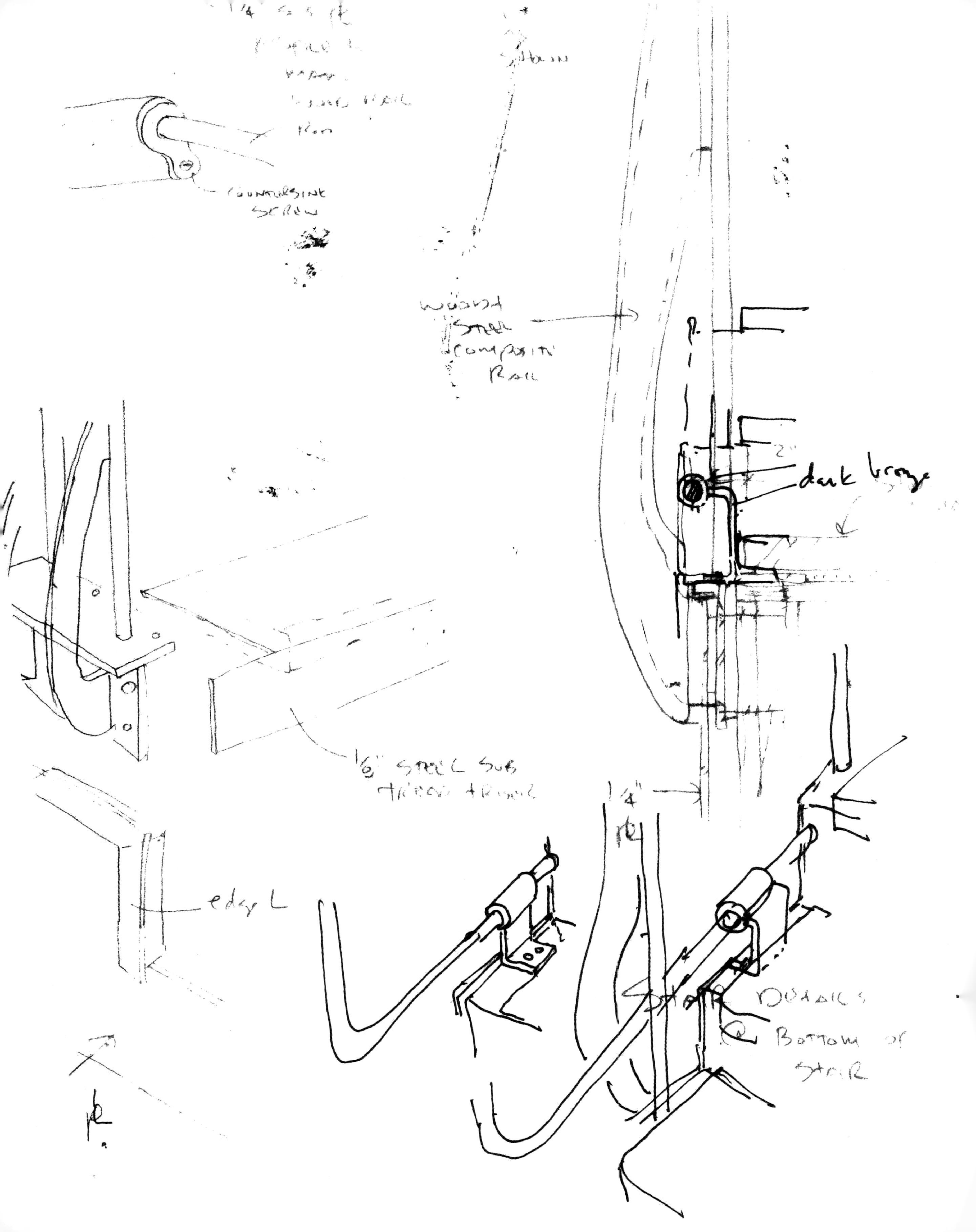
Rod
COUNTERSINK SCREW
RAIL
dark bronze
2"
1/8" STEEL SUB TREAD + RISER
1/4"
edge L
DETAILS @ BOTTOM OF STAIR

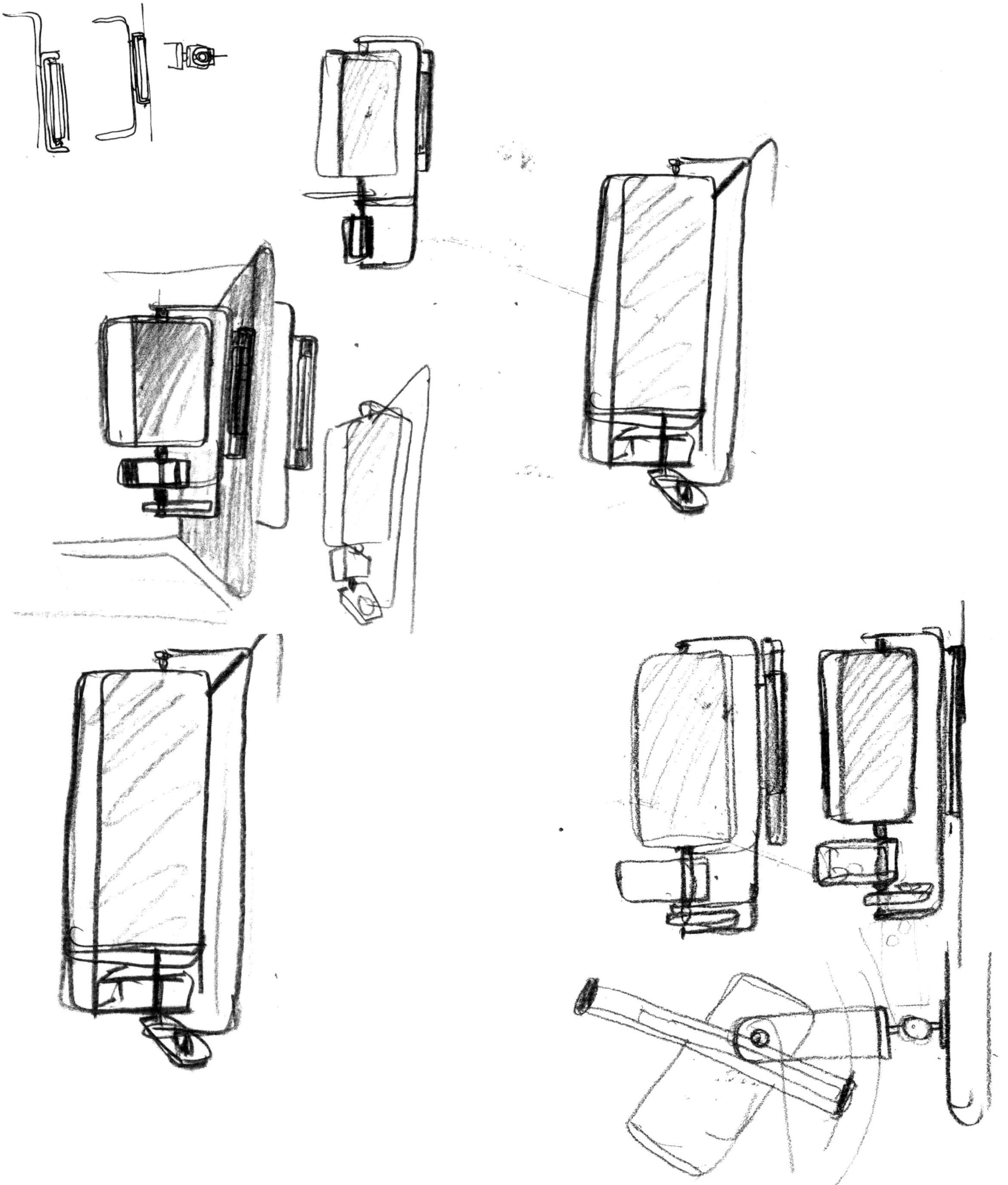

# The Garage

2015-2018

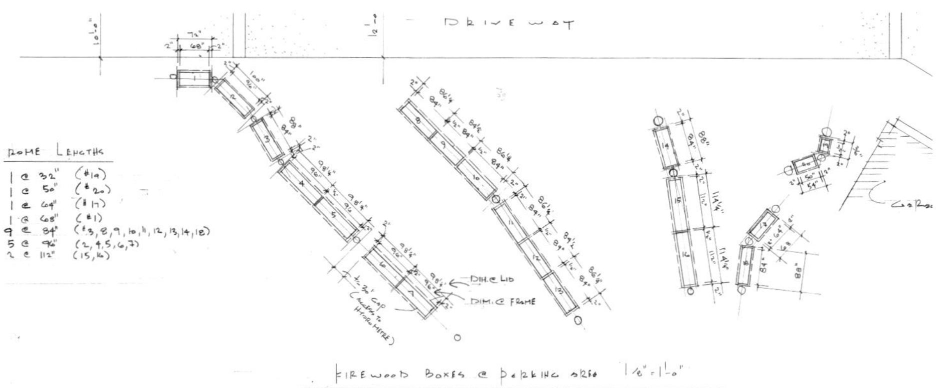


*Stacked wood walls defining parking area.*

The garage is the final building constructed at Point William and extends the design and construction strategies of the 1910 cottage. This is a pivotal building on the Point William site as it frames views of the cottage when you enter the clearing from the drive through the forest. Skylights cap a series of wood-lined coffers allowing natural light into the space. The building accommodates two cars, a workshop, and storage area. The weathering steel used for the guest cottage is echoed in the garage's roof and horizontal siding.

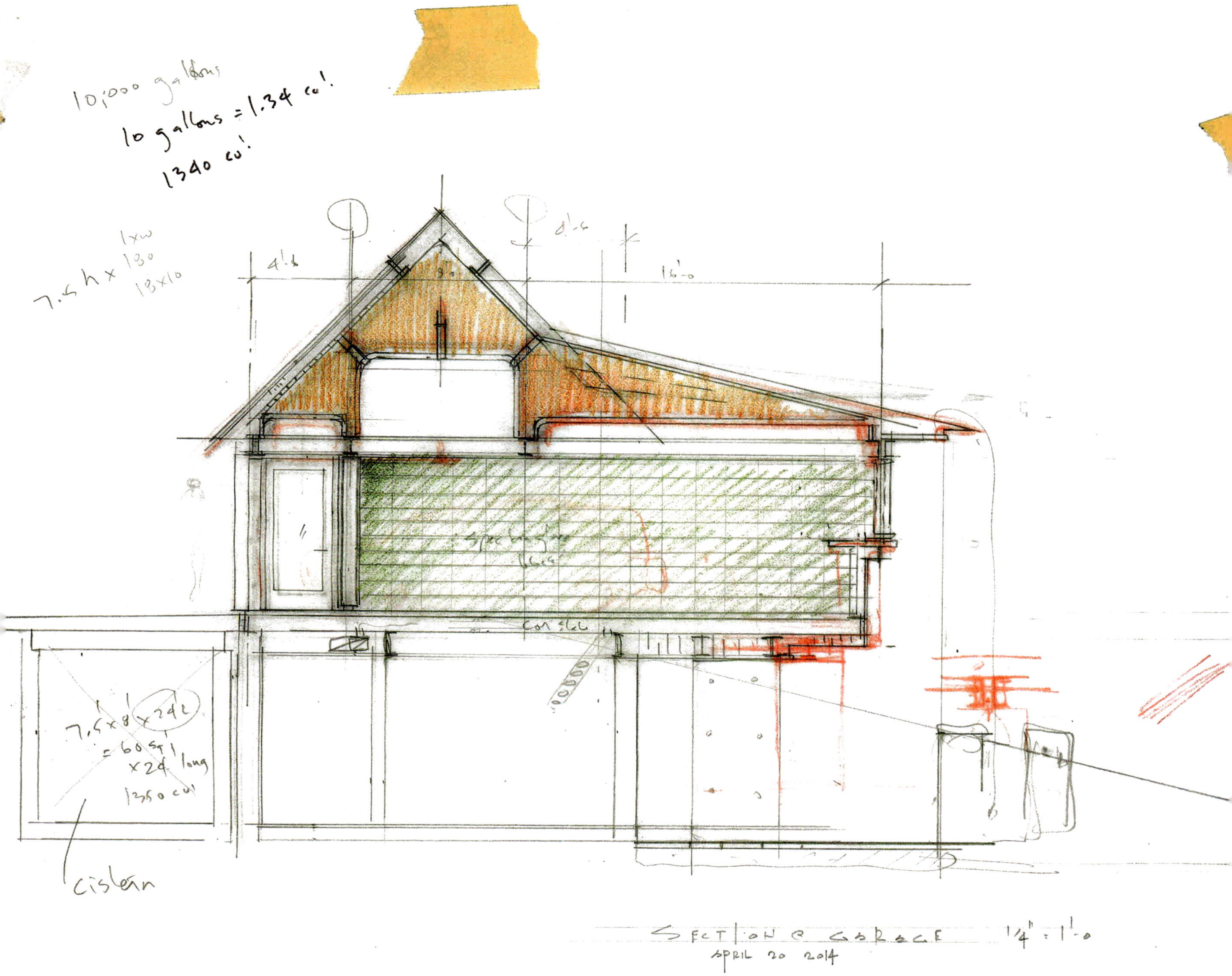
10,000 gallons
10 gallons = 1.34 cu!
1340 cu!
cistern
Section @ Garage 1/4" = 1'-0
April 20 2014

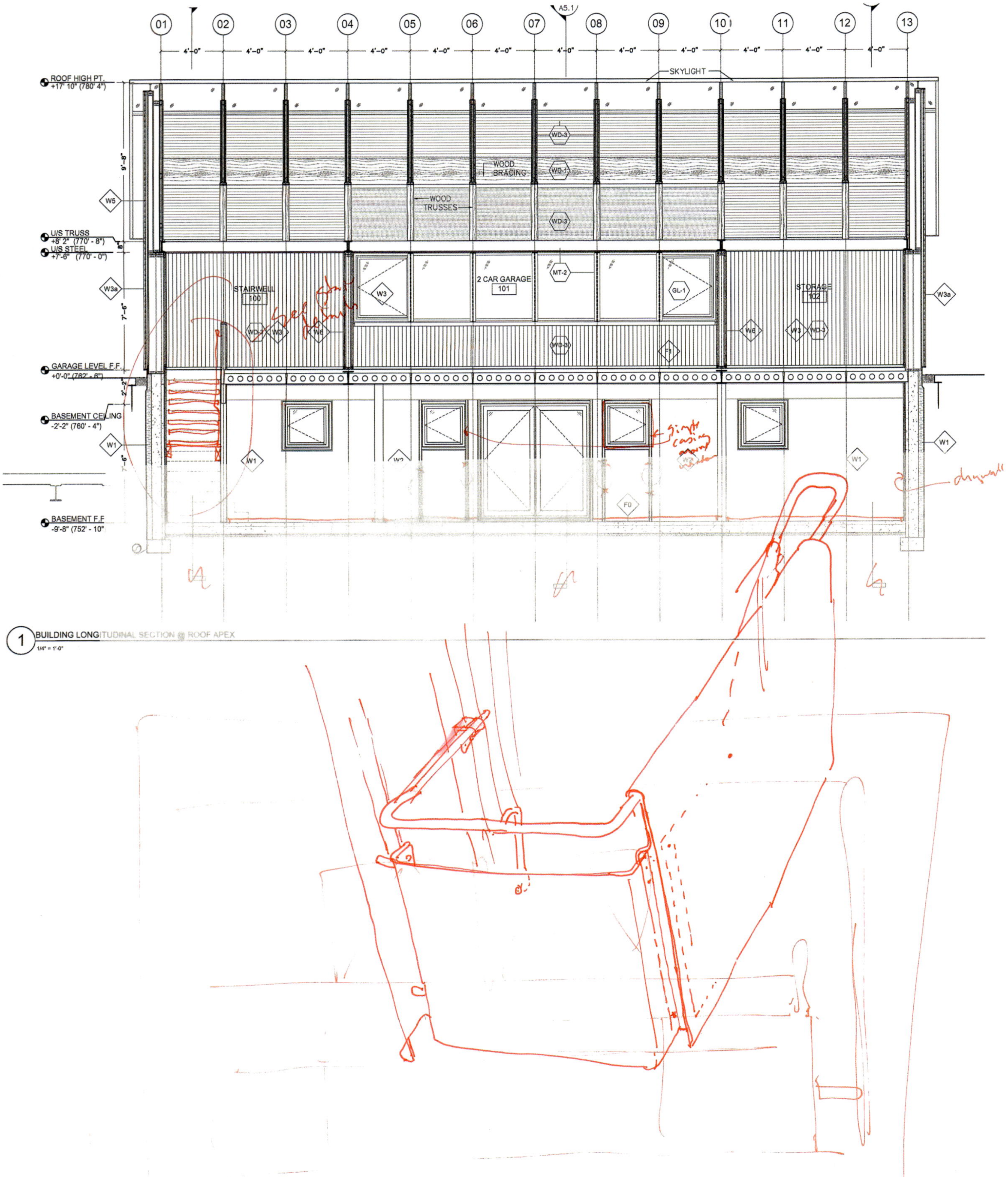
ROOF HIGH PT.
+17' 10" (780' 4")
U/S TRUSS
+8' 2" (770' - 8")
U/S STEEL
+7'-6" (770' - 0")
GARAGE LEVEL F.F.
+0'-0" (762' - 6")
BASEMENT CEILING
-2'-2" (760' - 4")
BASEMENT F.F
-9'-8" (752' - 10")
SKYLIGHT
WOOD BRACING
WOOD TRUSSES
STAIRWELL
100
2 CAR GARAGE
101
STORAGE
102
BUILDING LONGITUDINAL SECTION @ ROOF APEX
1/4" = 1'-0"

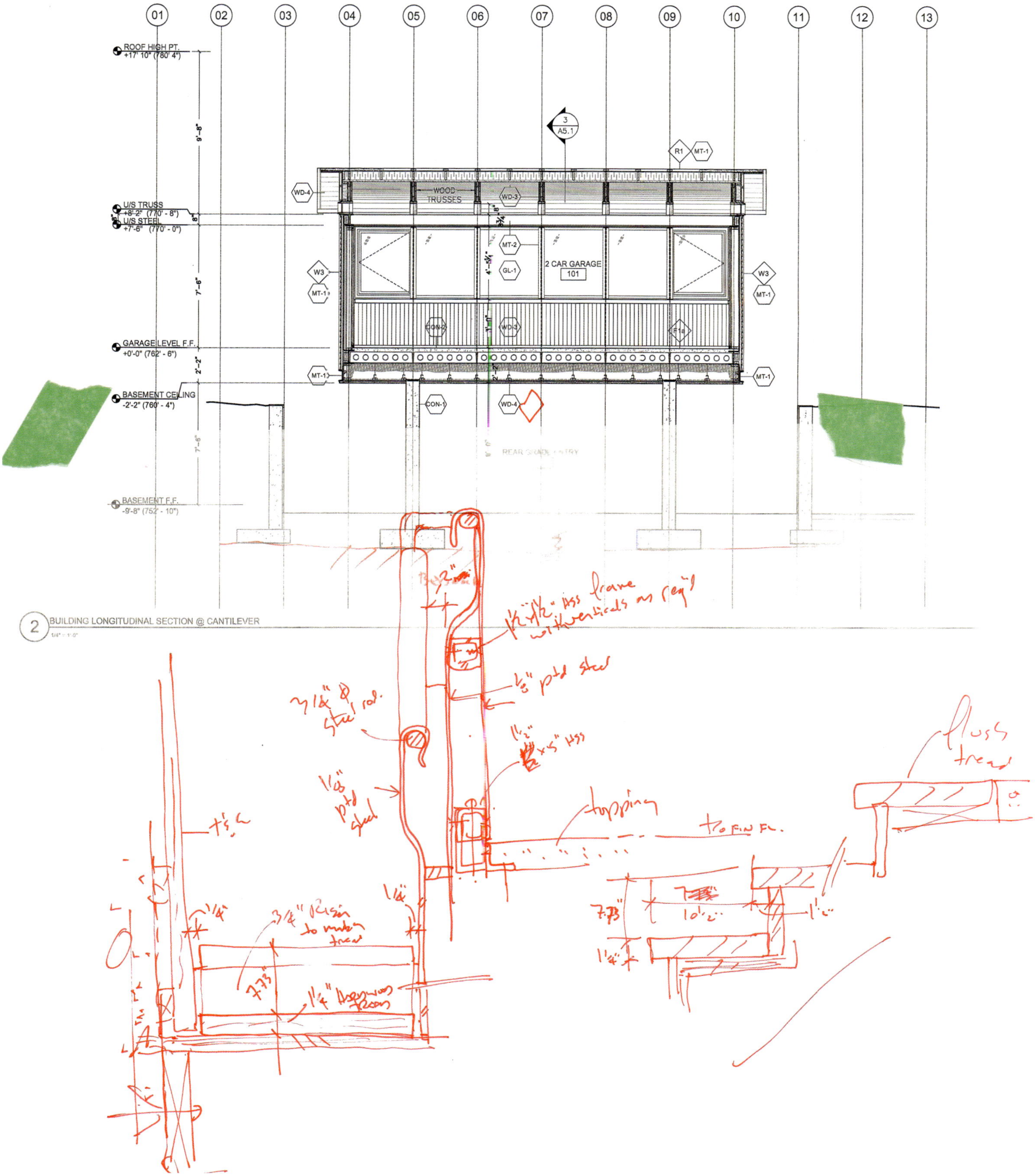
01
02
03
04
05
06
07
08
09
10
11
12
13
ROOF HIGH PT.
+17' 10" (780' 4")
U/S TRUSS
+8'-2" (770' - 8")
U/S STEEL
+7'-6" (770' - 0")
GARAGE LEVEL F.F.
+0'-0" (762' - 6")
BASEMENT CEILING
-2'-2" (760' - 4")
BASEMENT F.F.
-9'-8" (752' - 10")
WOOD TRUSSES
2 CAR GARAGE
101
REAR SHADE ENTRY
2 BUILDING LONGITUDINAL SECTION @ CANTILEVER

*The Point William cottage evolved over a twenty-year period from 1996–2018. This series of drawings and models document the metamorphosis of that evolution. After developing the first version of the cottage, we paused and that scheme was never built. Then we directed our energies to the design of the boathouse, which was developed quickly and built shortly afterwards. A decade later, we returned to design of the cottage as a new project with a program that combined the cottage with a guest cottage in one building.*

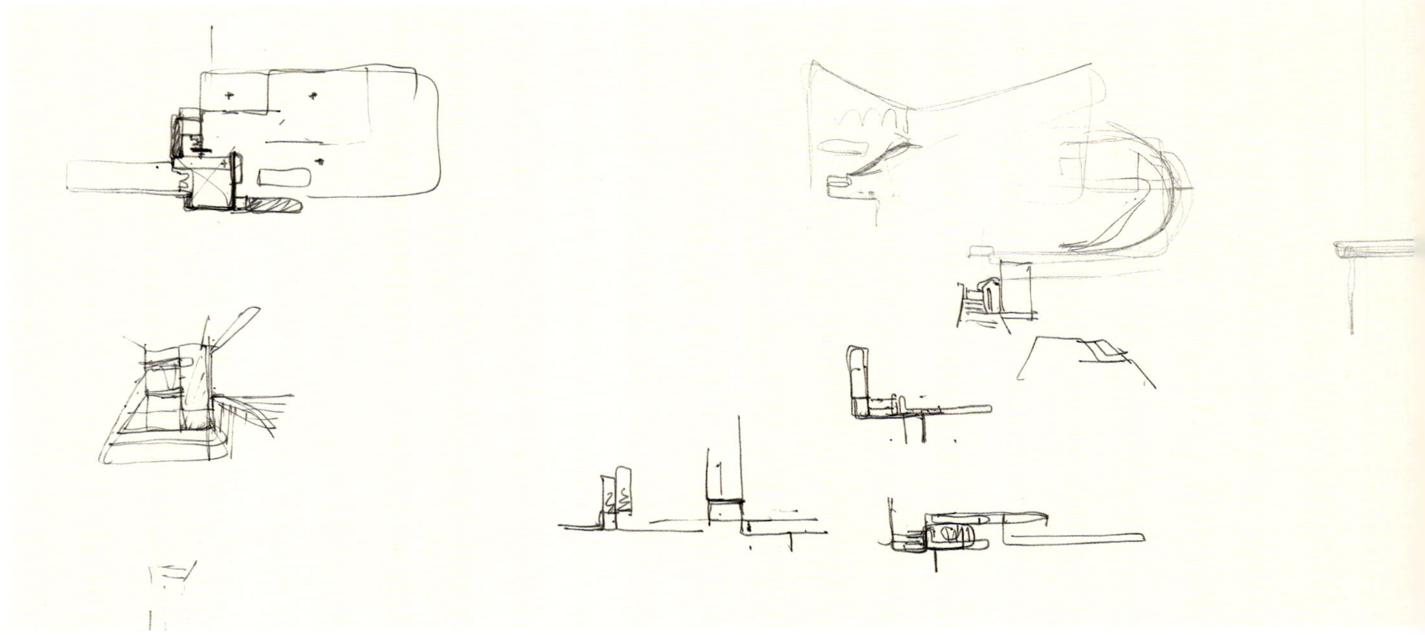

# A Laboratory for Living: The Evolution of Point William

Brigitte Shim and Howard Sutcliffe
in conversation with Michael Webb

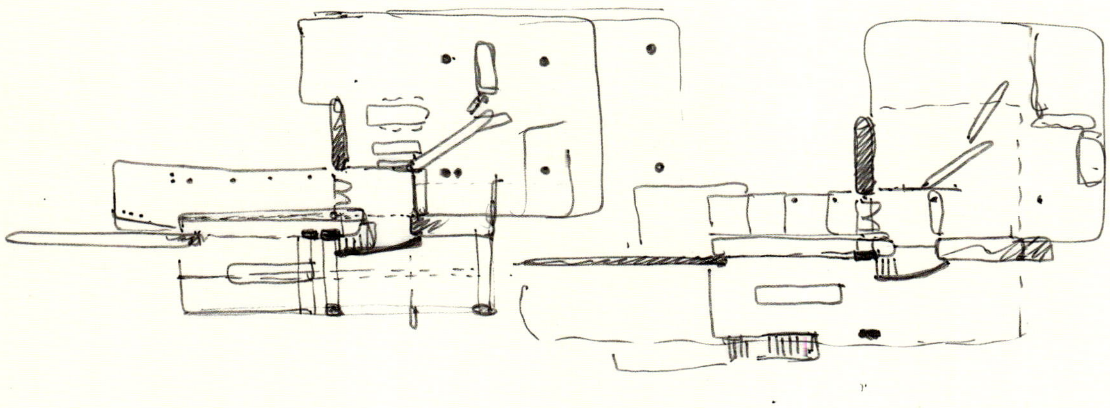

*(1996–1997) In this early plan variants, the main living spaces take the form of a rectangle and square, entered on the corner and arrived at by an extended entry sequence of columns, and steps. Inflected walls subdivide the main space and suggest a relationship between spaces. A linear portion of the building along the bottom (south) side of the plan is alluded to in both variations. The question of how you enter the cottage and how the spaces unfold is the investigation in these plans.*

The pleasure of making things permeates everything we do. Our work at Point William is a laboratory for living with many small-and large-scale experiments. The project evolved over two decades and transformed from the original design intentions into the ensemble of buildings and landscapes documented in this book.

Our involvement at Point William grew incrementally. In 1992, Toronto businessman Gerald Sheff invited several Canadian architects to compete for the commission of a new house in the city. Someone added our names to the list and we spent several months preparing our submission. We had just started our practice after working at other firms. Gerald awarded the house commission to Bruce Kuwabara, of KPMB Architects, which is just as well because we hadn't done anything nearly as ambitious. But he must have liked what we did because years later he and Shanitha Kachan asked us to look at a six-acre property on Lake Muskoka that he was contemplating buying. We drove up to the property and urged them to go for it. It felt like an island but was connected to the mainland and contained a 1960s house, along with a tumbledown turn-of-the-century cottage, a boat shelter, and garage.

Gerald's bid was accepted and we were invited to develop a master plan that would sever part of the property to create two lots. Reimagining the 1960s house was a challenge. Its monopitch roof and walls of cedar shingles blocked lake views. The master bed-

*In this plan, we were exploring the relationship between the entry at mid-level, the stair, and the fireplace mass. A large scale, half flight of stairs brings you up to the main floor by moving around the mass of the fireplace with the large landing at the top of the stairs affording views north. The kitchen overlooks the entry area, and a porch-like space extends to the south from the kitchen. Although essentially a linear plan, movement around the fireplace adds complexity to the spaces.*

room half-covered a dramatic granite outcrop. We prepared drawings and models to show how the new building could be pulled back from the granite outcrop, and secured planning approval for a linear plan on the footprint of the 1960s house when we applied for rezoning in 1997. The mandate was to set it thirty-five feet back from the shoreline; that mandatory setback has now been increased to sixty-six feet. So, the work we did long ago beforehand locked in the approval for when we did rebuild nearly twenty years later.

Gerald and Shanitha were willing to live in the existing house as it was, so we shifted our attention to the boathouse, adding a sleeping cabin above the indoor boat slips. Gerald and Shanitha described the accommodations they wanted as a "luxury Four Seasons Hotel suite over the water." This project gave us the opportunity to explore materials and design through the elements of lighting, hardware, furniture, and even boat cleats. At that time, we had only built a few things including a garden pavilion and reflecting pool, a house in Haliburton, and our own Laneway House in Toronto. For the boathouse we referenced the local vernacular: mahogany boats of the 1930s and the 1910 cottage on Point William with its cores and wraparound porch, as well as the Adirondack camps in upstate New York and Le Corbusier's rustic cabin in the south of France. Initially, we were going to use construction plywood as cladding, but, as the project became more sophisticated, we shifted to Douglas fir cladding combined with a heavy timber underwater

*This site and building study model examine diagonal movement through the center of the plan and an inflected stair from the entry area up toward the dining and living spaces. The fireplace (with an internal stair to loft above) creates a mass that separates entry from living. The private spaces of the cottage form a linear bar building extending to the left (west).*

infrastructure to support the boat house.

Gerald and Shanitha are open to the idea of life as a work of art and both are also interested in the design of all aspects of daily life. Gerald completed a degree in architecture at McGill and practiced for five years before making his career in real estate and, ultimately, investment management. He wanted to enjoy every stage of the design and construction process. We received bids for construction from a local contractor, Wayne Judges, as well as two Toronto firms. After tightening the program, we went with Wayne and he continued to work on all of the projects at Point William. This first job was done incrementally, giving the owners time to make choices. We explained to the clients that a galvanized metal roof would work but might be viewed as too shiny from across the lake, so eventually we went with a more mellow zinc roof. Gerald insisted on the highest quality but always joked, "We gave them an unlimited budget and they exceeded it."

After creating an outdoor firepit and gathering place in the interim, ten years later we rebuilt the guest cottage. The guest cottage provided Gerald and Shanitha with somewhere to live while the 1960s house was rebuilt, and the boathouse became their summer retreat from their extended family. They created an opportunity for a young architect to design a tree house for the grandchildren in the form of a student competition held at the architecture school at the University of Toronto. We were very lucky

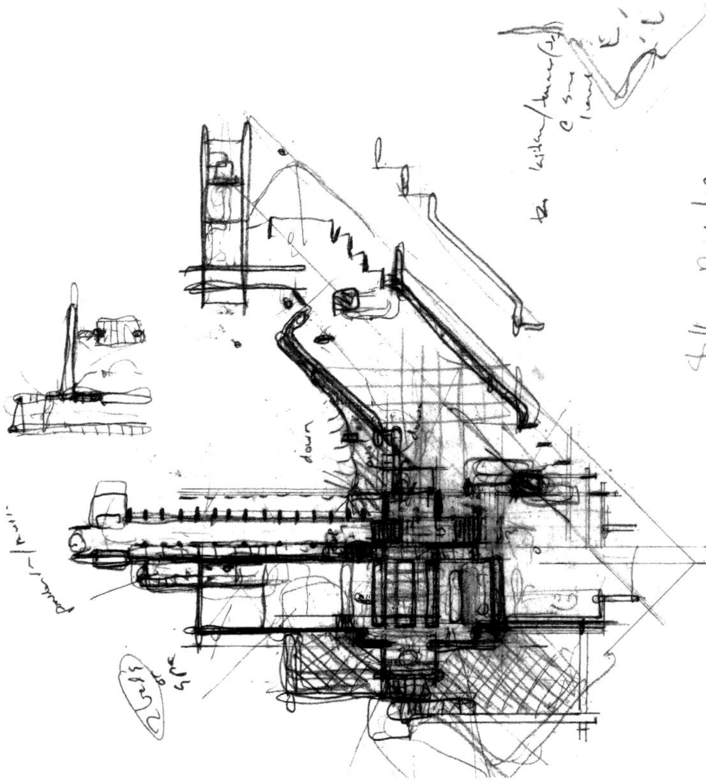

*In this intermediate variant, we explored the possibility of unifying the new cottage with the guest cottage through a large loggia-like space. The 45-degree line of this space followed the shoreline closely and wrapped around the large outcropping of rock behind.*

to meet Tom Montgomery, a skilled master carpenter working for Wayne. He built most of the projects at Point William including the winning treehouse design by Lukasz Kos. Another well-respected architectural firm, Kohn Shnier Architects, designed a successful two-family cottage located on the severed property adjacent to Point William for Gerald's daughters, Rhonda and Laurie, and their families.

In redesigning the guest cottage, we turned its constraints to advantage. The zoning agreement for two residential units on a single property mandated that we not increase the height or enlarge the footprint of the 1910 cabin and that we retain its form and silhouette. We were equally determined to preserve its original, vernacular character while relating to other buildings on site including a new cottage, which was a probability though not a certainty at that time. We also sketched a composite scheme that linked the guest cottage to a new cottage with a loggia, but that was rejected by the planning department. We were limited to the two original footprints on the site and the agreed setback from the lake.

The architectural language of forms and materials for the guest cottage was drawn from the boathouse. We tried to maintain the feeling of a porch in the kitchen and dining room, and the underside of the ceiling indicates whether you are in the inner or outer part of the building. Stairs lead from the main living spaces around the fireplace and up to the bedrooms on the second floor in a pinwheel plan. The exterior

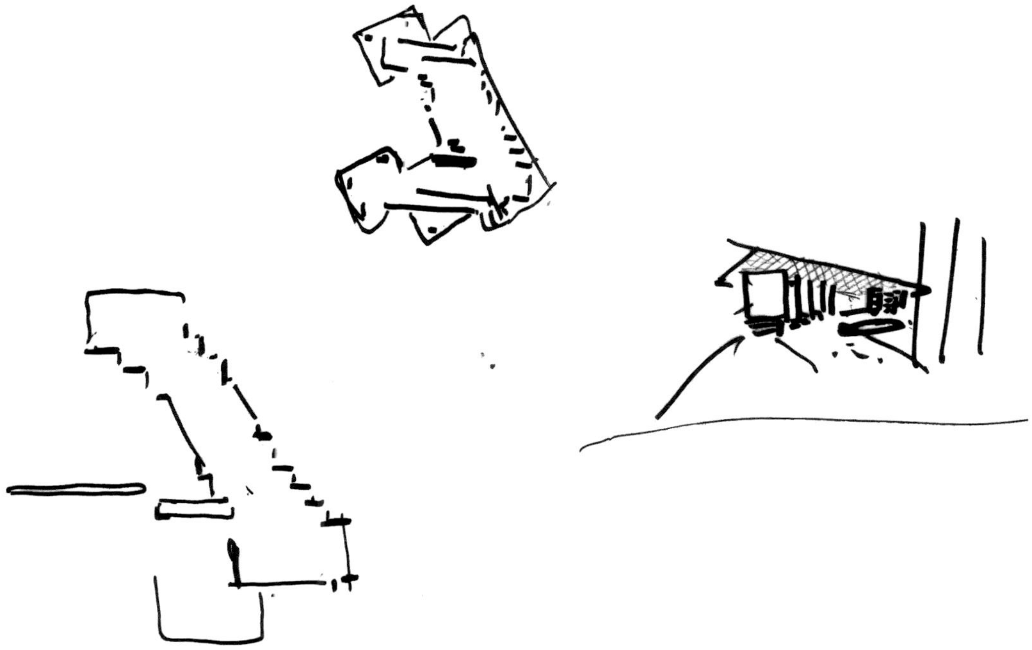

*These sketches examine the form of the central space between the two existing buildings, the 1910 cabin and 1960s house, and looks at the expression of the fins or pier-like elements. This space in between the two existing buildings uses the pier-like elements to frame views of the water and landscape beyond.*

porch of the guest cottage serves as a threshold for the descent to the boat house and it is a pivotal point from which you can see the other buildings on the site.

By the time we finished the guest cottage, the roof of the 1960s house had sprung leaks—a providential warning. Erasure of a portion of the existing house revealed the beauty of the granite outcrop. It also provided much-needed breathing room between the two buildings and a view of the lake. Gerald and Shanitha gave us the go-ahead and we designed the new cottage to be understated and opaque to the lake by day. As you approach it appears to be the smallest building on the site. You feel as if you are entering an outdoor porch that is more exterior than interior. Bays are cantilevered and feel as though they are floating above the ground, along with the canopies that shade and protect windows and outdoor terraces. The new house is 3,500 square feet on the main floor and 3,000 square feet on the lower level.

To break up the mass, and to articulate the distinct interior spaces, we used specific exterior materials such as weathering steel, local stone walls, and ipe wood, enduring materials that will weather well. In between the steel fins and stone are the glass panels that reveal the living spaces. Irregularly spaced steel-clad mullions along the glazed porch/entry gallery create a syncopated rhythm. The 1960s house had a monopitch roof sloping down toward the water. We reversed that with a curved roof that embraces views of lake and sky and pulls in abundant natural

The ideas of the formal geometry of the plans as a parallel idea of the construction methodology were developing in these plans. The idea of using heavy timber in log cabin-like construction was an exploration we had started in the boathouse project, and here it was developed more emphatically. An expressed deep timber grid was imagined for the roof /ceiling plane that would give a clear visible order to the project. This plan variant was abandoned due to the zoning implications.

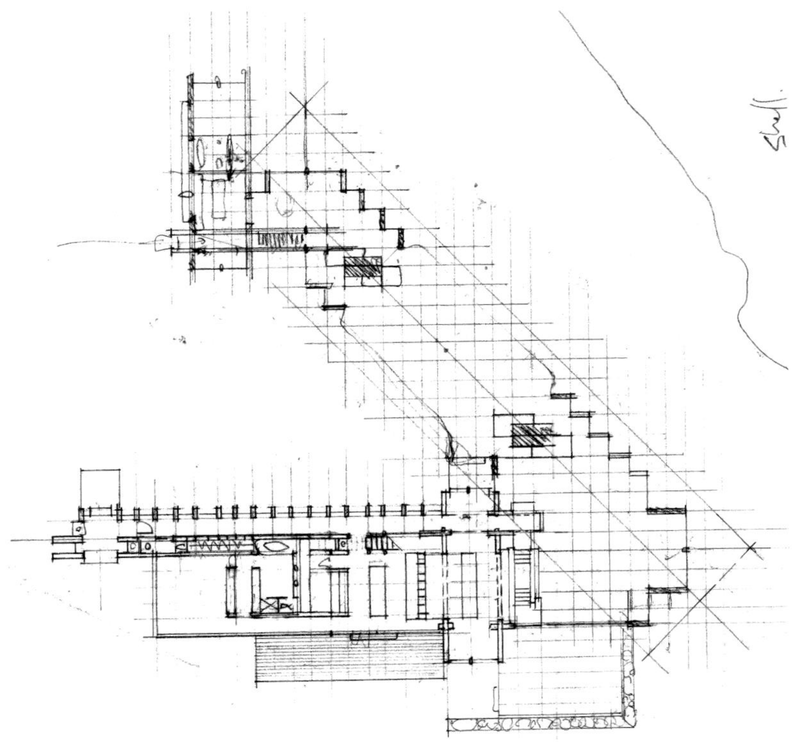

light. It engages in a dialogue with the guest cottage and frames views of the landscape without overwhelming it.

For Gerald and Shanitha, the functional aspect—how spaces relate to each other—is critical and also a legacy of Gerald's architectural education at McGill in the 1960s. Looking along the length of the cottage now, from the entry and out to the lake, we see a strong sense of axiality, a playing off of a series of short-cross axes. The whole cottage is a succession of surprises unfolding cinematically. Different scales of design investigations are juxtaposed and spaces are orchestrated and recalibrated, with soaring gathering spaces contrasted with more intimate areas. A sequence of rooms, from the master suite to the dining room, form a linear core and these interior enclosures are faced with exterior weathering steel. The fluidity of the interior is emphasized by the watery pattern of granite floors and sensual rounded windows. Overhangs shade the glass from high sun and reflections from the lake shimmer off the underside of the ceiling. Bowed wooden ceilings bring in afternoon light from the west and a skylight over the stairs pulls light into the lower floor.

The boathouse inspired the selection of materials used in the cottage. Boldly grained Douglas fir clads the ceilings adjacent to the straight-grain Douglas fir used in the paneling and cabinetry. Granite introduces a new element and integral ornament in the tradition of Adolf Loos. We used the same Canadian granite, quarried in Quebec, with three different finishes: leathered on the floors, flamed on the hearths—where the tone shifts to pale gray—and rough-hewn granite stone on exterior walls. One of these exterior walls

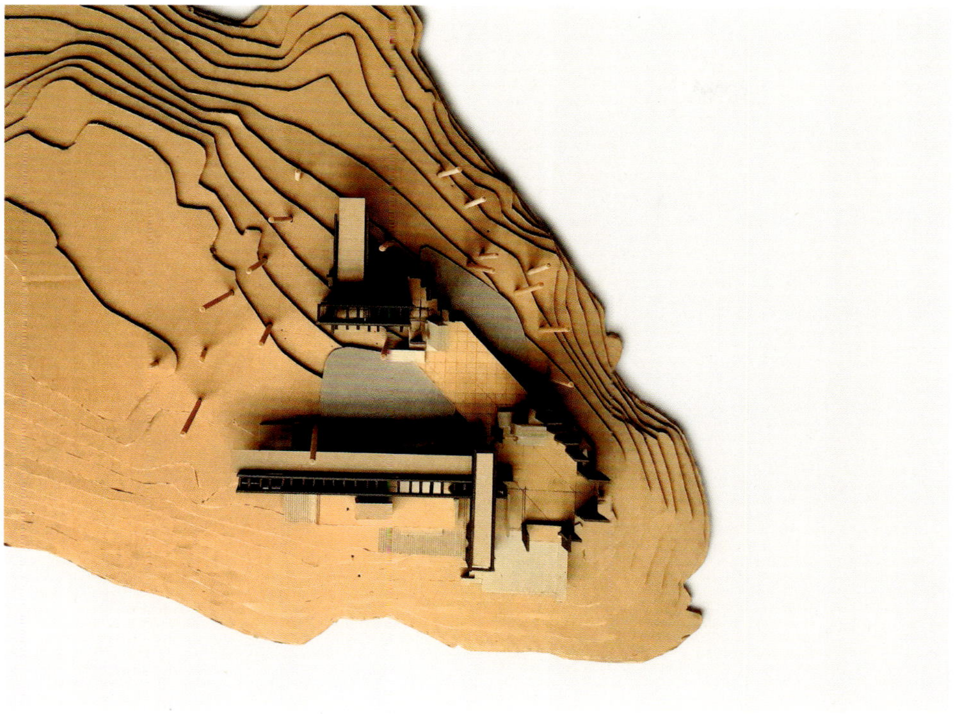

*This site and building model continue the design exploration of the linking of the two existing buildings with a porch space in between. This space situated between the rock and the water connects you to the landscape. The model interrogates the building's relationship to the site further.*

is framed by an expansive glass slider in the master shower, evoking the glacier-scoured outcrop beside the entry. Curved wood ceilings, sculptured door handles, and a tactile stair balustrade all evoke the work of Alvar Aalto, and especially his Villa Mairea in Finland. Point William is a mediation between curvilinear and orthogonal, much more understated and subtly shaped than our Integral House in Toronto, which is all curves and was completed a few years earlier.

We designed all the built-ins, fittings, and some new furnishings to complement Gerald and Shanitha's collection of rustic, classic, modern furniture. Our design work includes the dining room credenza, a bronze and wood dining table, and three lamps mounted on wire hoops over the dining room table that can be re-oriented to address regular dining or rotated to embrace large family gatherings. The organic-shaped suspended, 3-D printed lamp over the kitchen table was developed independently. Its undulating shape has an affinity with an Inuit whalebone sculpture in the guest cottage. Bronze door handles were inspired by the architectural section through the living space of the cottage. Several of the door handles nestle into recesses we fondly call the handle coffins. The door handles, the bronze up-lights, and a set of steel fire irons were crafted by combining 3-D-printed metal with handcrafted elements to serve as functional sculptures that animate unornamented surfaces.

A bigger cottage gives one the opportunity to create complex spatial relationships. A villa we recently completed in Moscow explores similar spatial ideas as Point William but on a larger scale. The pairing of projects and the intense dialogue between them often

*This sketch is one of the first sketches for the third and final variant of the cottage on the site of the 1960s house. It explores large pinwheeling walls that frame the landscape in different ways from each quadrant, allowing for multiple aspects of the site to be articulated and an implied extension from interior space out to the exterior in all directions.*

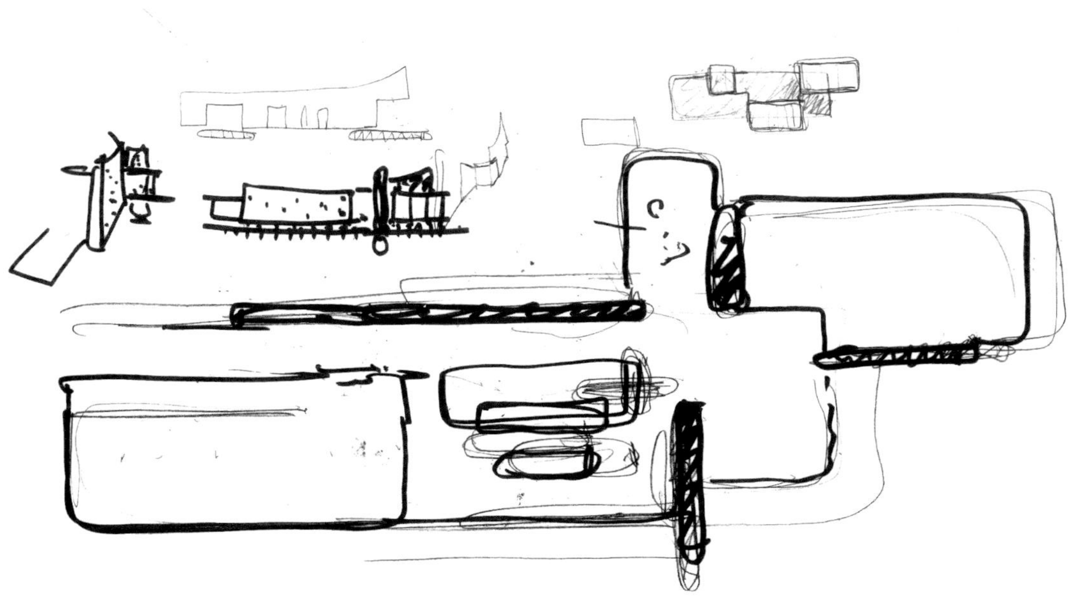

occurs in our work and then we move on in another direction. We call these kinds of projects "cousins." For example, this pairing also occurred when we were designing Glen and Susan Lowry's house in Quebec at the same time as we were constructing our own retreat on Harrison Island in Georgian Bay. When the Lowrys visited our place they remarked on the spatial resonances between the two rectilinear structures despite their differences.

The trusting relationship we built with Gerald and Shanitha over many years enabled us to explore ideas at the varied scales of building, landscape, furniture, fittings, and fixtures. Our work at Point William is an evolution and an on-going investigation into the ways that design can impact and contribute to everyday life. The extensive use of a boldly patterned granite, with rich tones that play off the natural shades of the walls and ceilings, is a strong move creating a symphony of color and pattern. Bringing the outside in with the weathering steel cladding of the core was the biggest stretch for the clients. Stone is the unifying material, but we wanted a contrast as you approach the water, and so the granite yields to large precast concrete panels, polished to reflect light. As ideas flowed between buildings they also read together as an ensemble. Each building at Point William is different but there are resonances and an echoing from one to another.

The cottage alternates between rough and refined, plain and patterned surfaces throughout. A glazed wall works its way sinuously through the cottage, its fluid lines and rounded corners turning the glass into a lens that distorts and refracts the landscape view at moments of transition. We explored the role of light, which is pulled into the cottage from many different

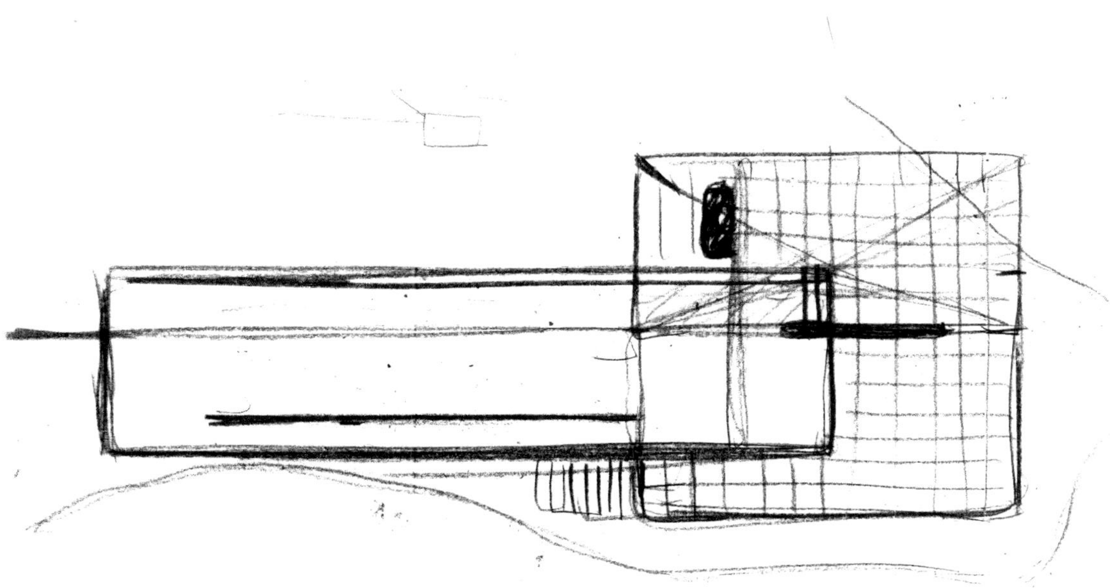

*In this plan, we are examining a linear bar scheme that intersects with a square, terrace-like living space, set a few steps down from the entry hall minimally described here by the line extending from the wall in the living space. This sketch examines program distribution, with entry sequence parallel to the linear building mass, and views to the lake beyond the living room framed by the fireplace mass. The relationship of rooms and spaces in this plan is relatively consistent with the completed project.*

directions, to wash surfaces, to reflect off others, and to bounce up to the ceiling. The whole building is a light box, constantly changing through the day and bringing spaces to life. That's one of the fundamental aspects of our work—magical transformations, subtle variations, dramatic shifts between seasons, and materials that register and amplify the light.

The garage was the last project to be completed. The old garage was in even worse shape than the former 1960s house so we told Gerald and Shanitha that they needed to replace it. We designed the new structure as a background building with similar features to the guest cottage: a log storage wall alternating with horizontal steel cladding and a steel roof along with deep roof beams to shape the garage's interior, which is used for parties, ping pong, and other functions besides stabling cars. The garage is the first building you see as you drive onto the property and it is an important threshold revealing the tip of Point William. We wanted you to feel as though it had always been there.

Our relationship with Gerald and Shanitha is a special one, and it's not the first time we've achieved a double portrait in a house. What clients tell you they want and what they describe as their program is not always the same. You have to get under the skin of a client and you always need to listen carefully to the way they express themselves. Sometimes, the words articulated and what they actually mean to the client can be two different things. It's the paradox of being an architect: people come to you for what they want and you do what you want.

A linear bar of program space surrounded by emphatic porch-like space on three sides, articulated by a fin glazing wall. At the end of the top hall, or porch space, and large terrace-like living space overlooking the lake. The central bar contains the private aspects of the program as well as the service components.

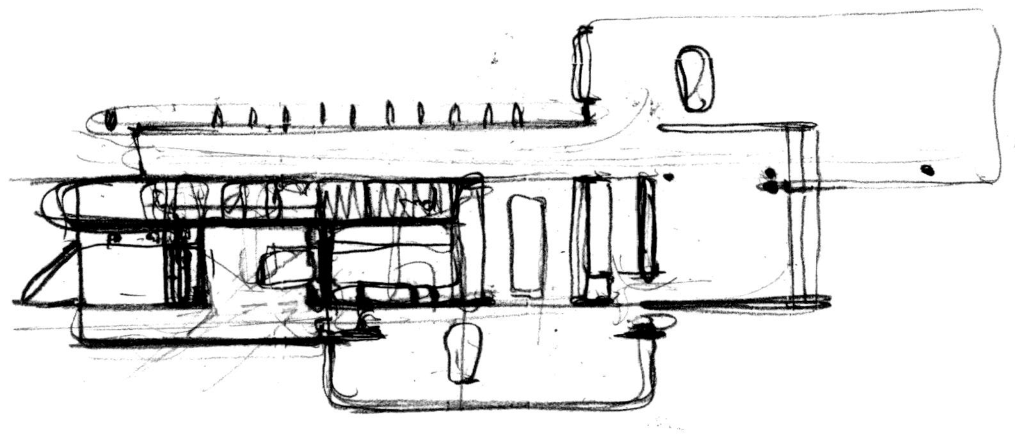

This happened before with our first clients Murray and Barbara Frum on their Toronto ravine property. Barbara was a probing journalist and when we met you always felt you were being interrogated. She never said "no" to anything, but she was always curious and asked lots of questions. This was good training, for working with Gerald and Shanitha who are both curious and engaged in how things are made. One of the things we learned early on working with them is that if you didn't know the answer to a question you simply said, "I don't know but I will get back to you."

We were in charge of designing the landscape at Point William and worked with local landscaping contractor Rick Wright to achieve our design for the site. The biggest move was to bend the driveway at the edge of the meadow that covers the septic tank so that it turns to reveal the house. Gravel, edged with shaped curvilinear steel, was laid to demarcate the boundary of the drive and entry court. Forest surrounds the meadow, leading your eyes on to the exposed rock outcropping, which becomes a found object in the landscape. We planted a lot of native specimens to complement the mature white pines.

Serendipity and timing played a major role in our work at Point William. We built the smallest piece of the program first, and the largest third. If the cottage had come first it would have been a very different project, because it would have had to accommodate children and grandchildren when they came to stay. Once a two-family cottage was completed on the adjoining property, the cottage had a different program: a couple who like to entertain. What you don't want is a huge space that you rattle around in when you are on

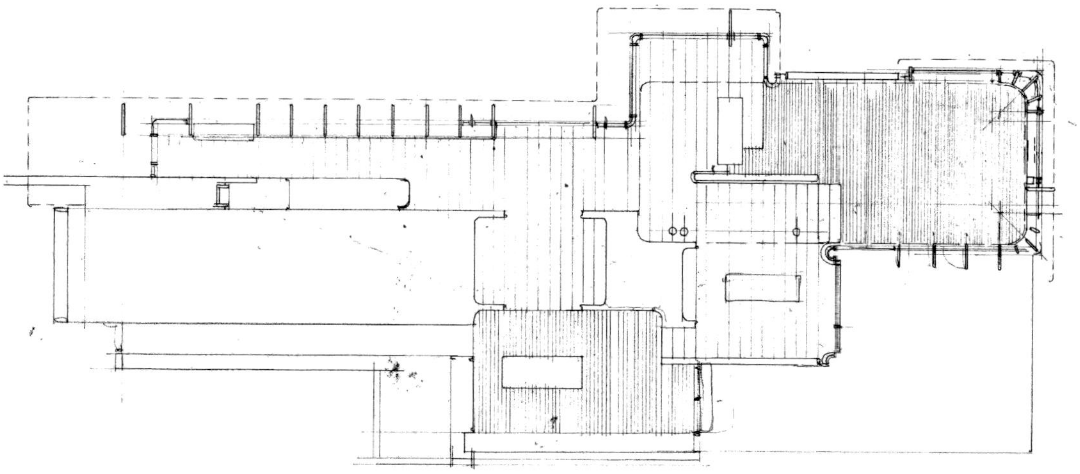

*This plan, drawn late in the development of the project, examines the roll of the glazing system as a continuous undulating line, wrapping around much of the cottage. Folding in on itself in the inside corners and radiused at the outside corners, the glass oscillates between lens-like object and transparent opening. In parallel with this glazing line, corners of walls in rooms are radiused and in contrast to the radius glass corners, which extend the panoramic condition of the glass, the corners in the walls create a more embracing gesture.*

your own, but there are times when you need a place for large family gatherings. The cottage now provides a combination of grand and intimate spaces that work for one person, for the expanding younger generation of the family, and for large gatherings. The program for our project in Moscow is similar to that of the Point William project, resulting in a variety of spaces of different scales and a good fit to the site within a mature pine forest.

Even though Gerald and Shanitha are an intensely urban couple, they have fallen in love with Point William and often spend time there in late fall and through the winter when no one else is around. As our clients spent more and more time at Point William, it enabled them to precisely articulate what they needed.

The passages of time between the buildings at Point William was a critical factor allowing us to deepen our understanding of the site. At the outset, when you arrived at the site you couldn't see the water because the buildings were jammed together, so the act of erasure was as important as the act of rebuilding. All of the buildings are engaged in a conversation with each other as well as with the landscape and with the site and there are views that were previously hidden that are now revealed. At Point William, each new building is built roughly on the footprint of its predecessor. One building responds to the next and the landscape stitches the whole thing together. When carefully assembled, built form and landscape have the potential to create meaningful and memorable places in the Canadian landscape. Our episodic journey reimagining Point William revealed to us that the open spaces created between buildings are as important as the design of the individual buildings.

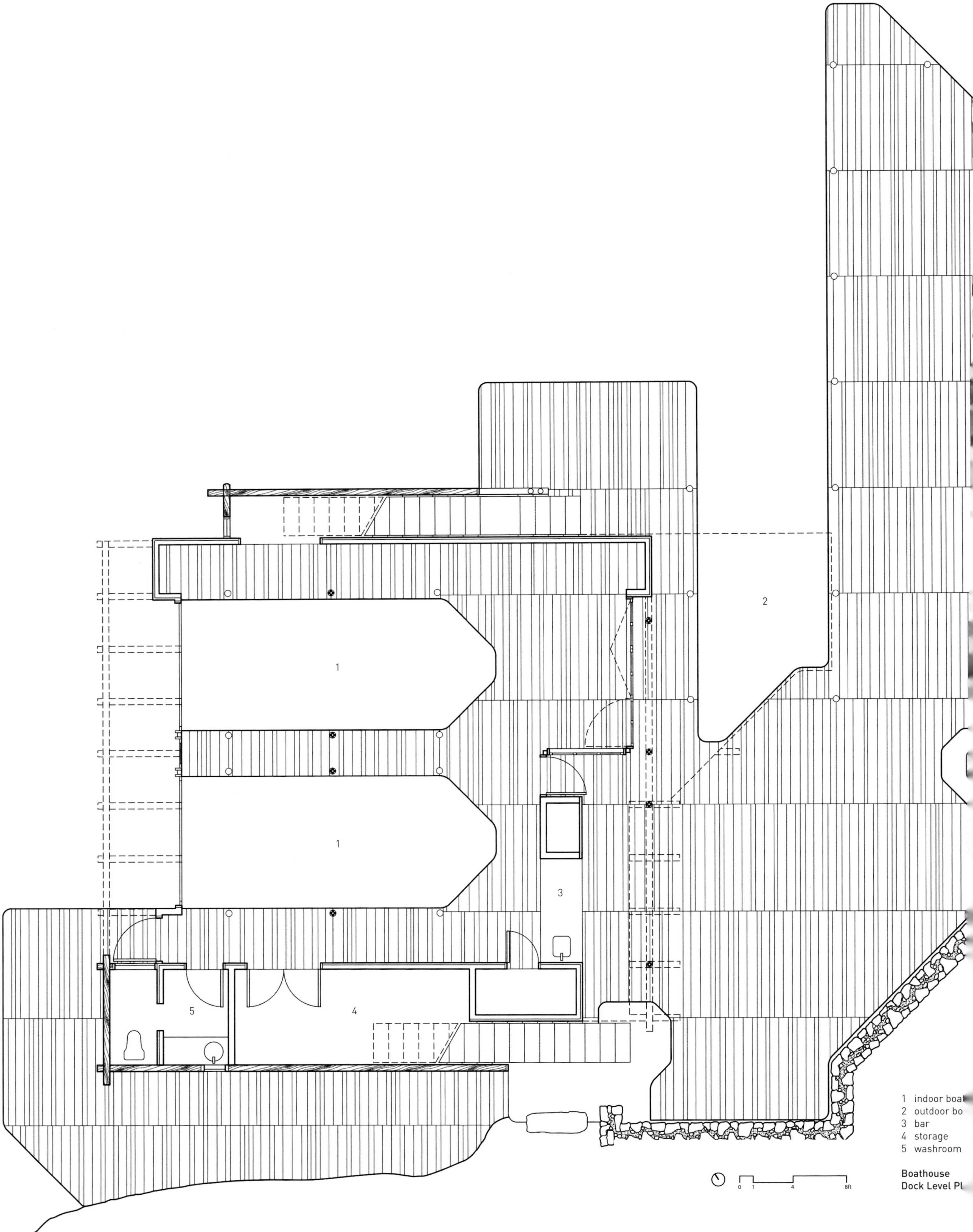


1 indoor boa
2 outdoor bo
3 bar
4 storage
5 washroom

**Boathouse**
**Dock Level Pl**

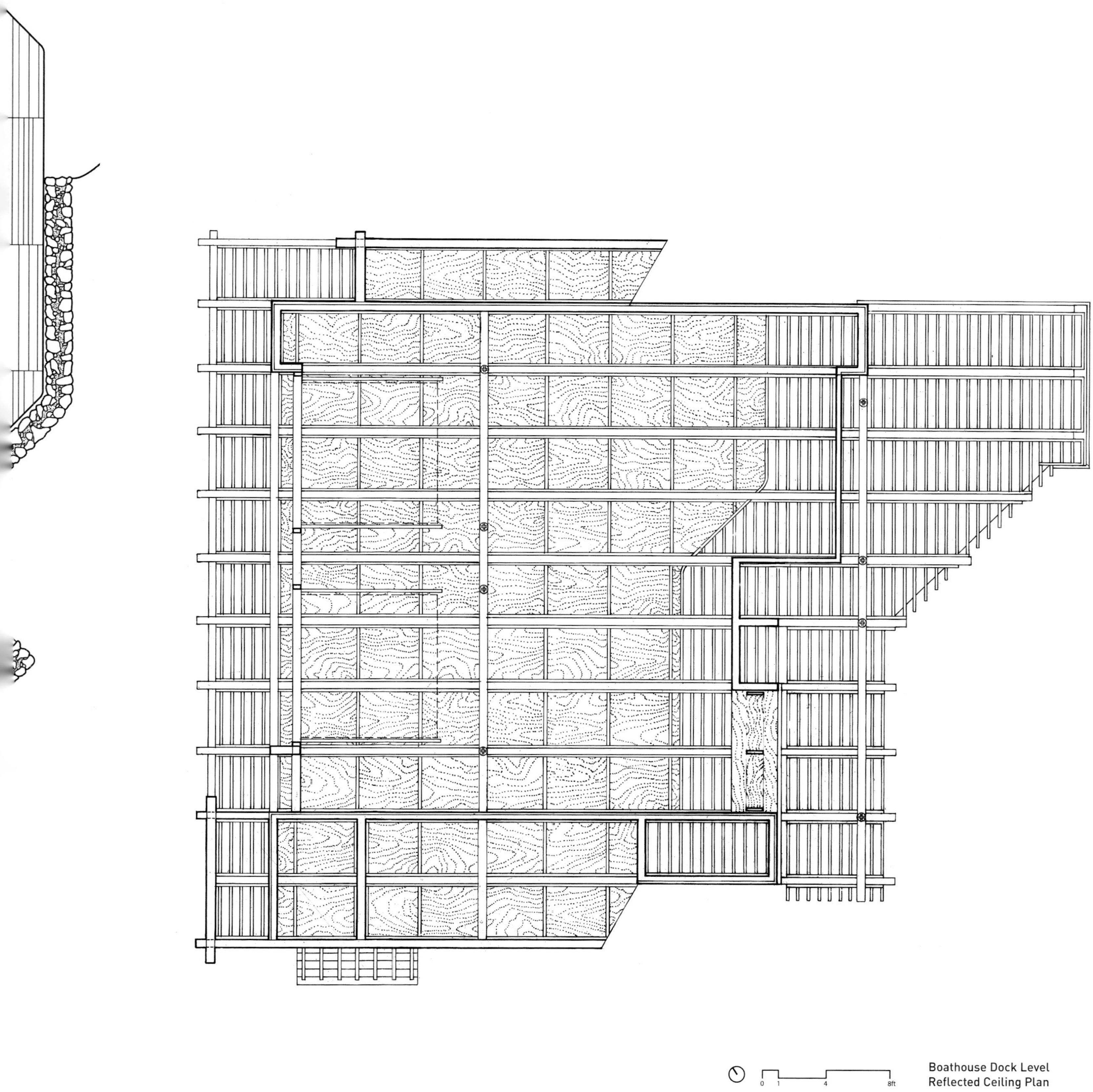


Boathouse Dock Level
Reflected Ceiling Plan

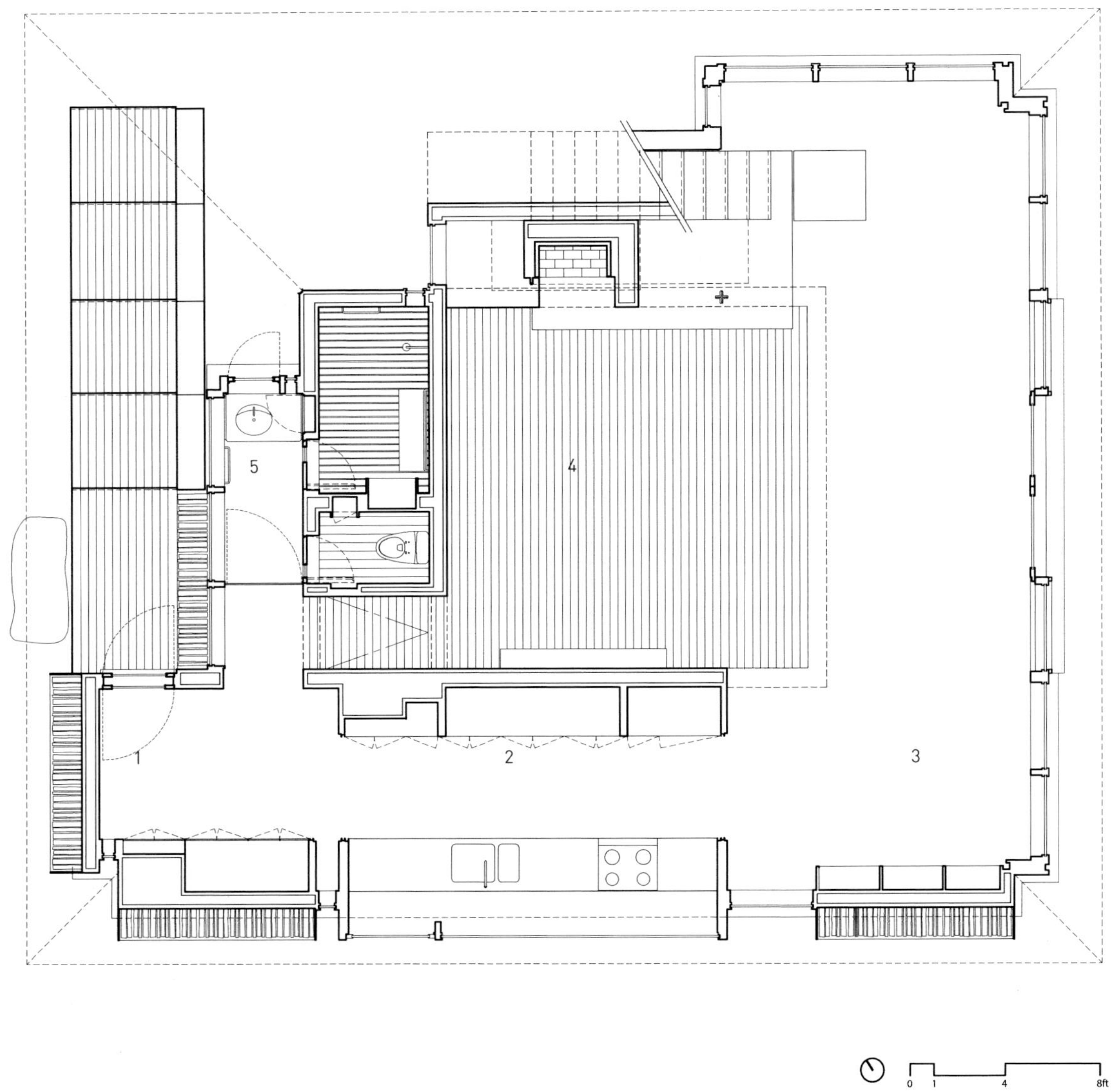


1 entry/porch
2 kitchen/porch
3 dining/porch
4 living
5 bathroom

**Guest Cottage**
**Ground Floor Plan**

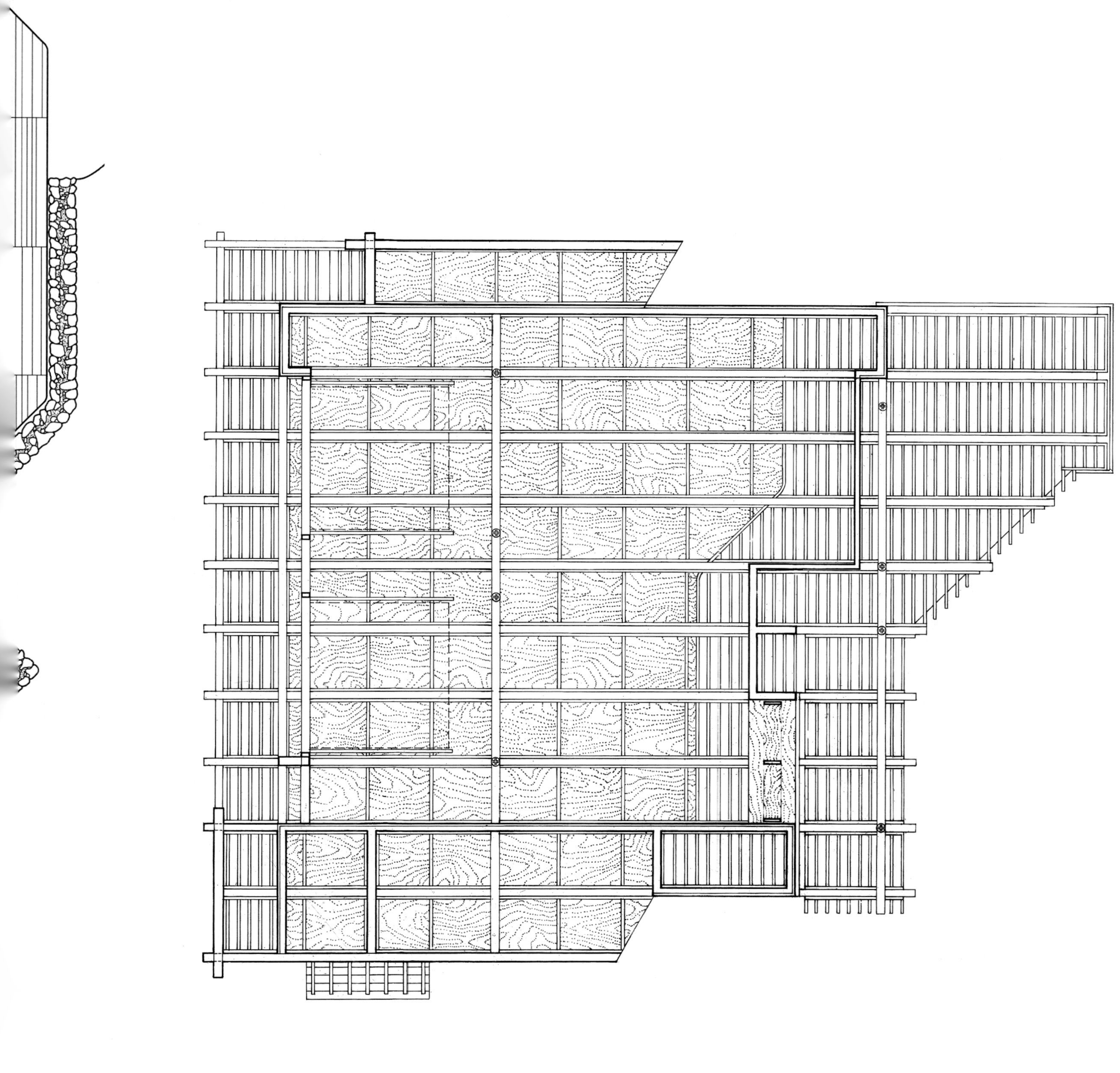

Boathouse Dock Level
Reflected Ceiling Plan

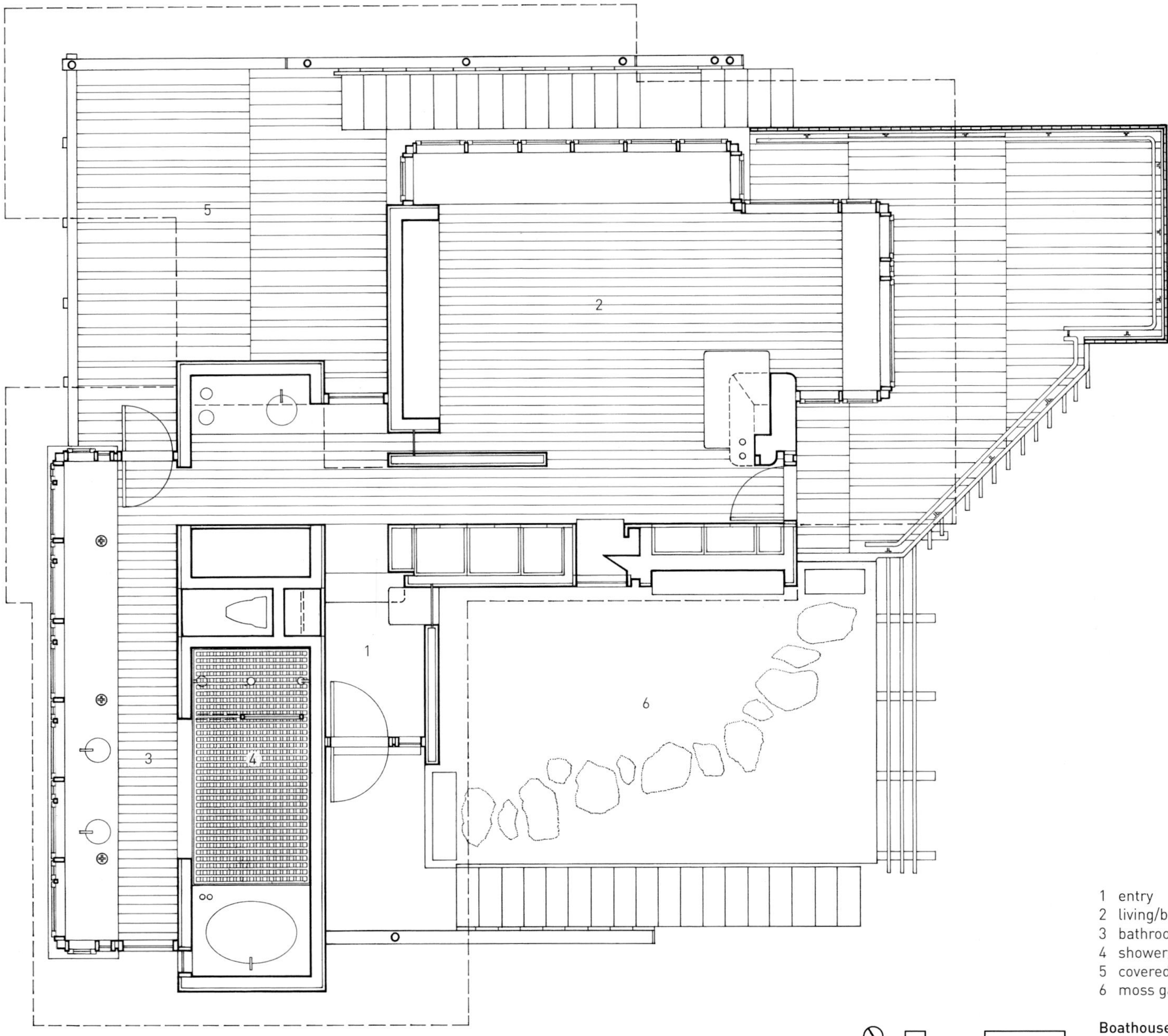


1 entry
2 living/bedroom
3 bathroom
4 shower/tub
5 covered deck
6 moss garden

**Boathouse**
**Second Floor Plan**

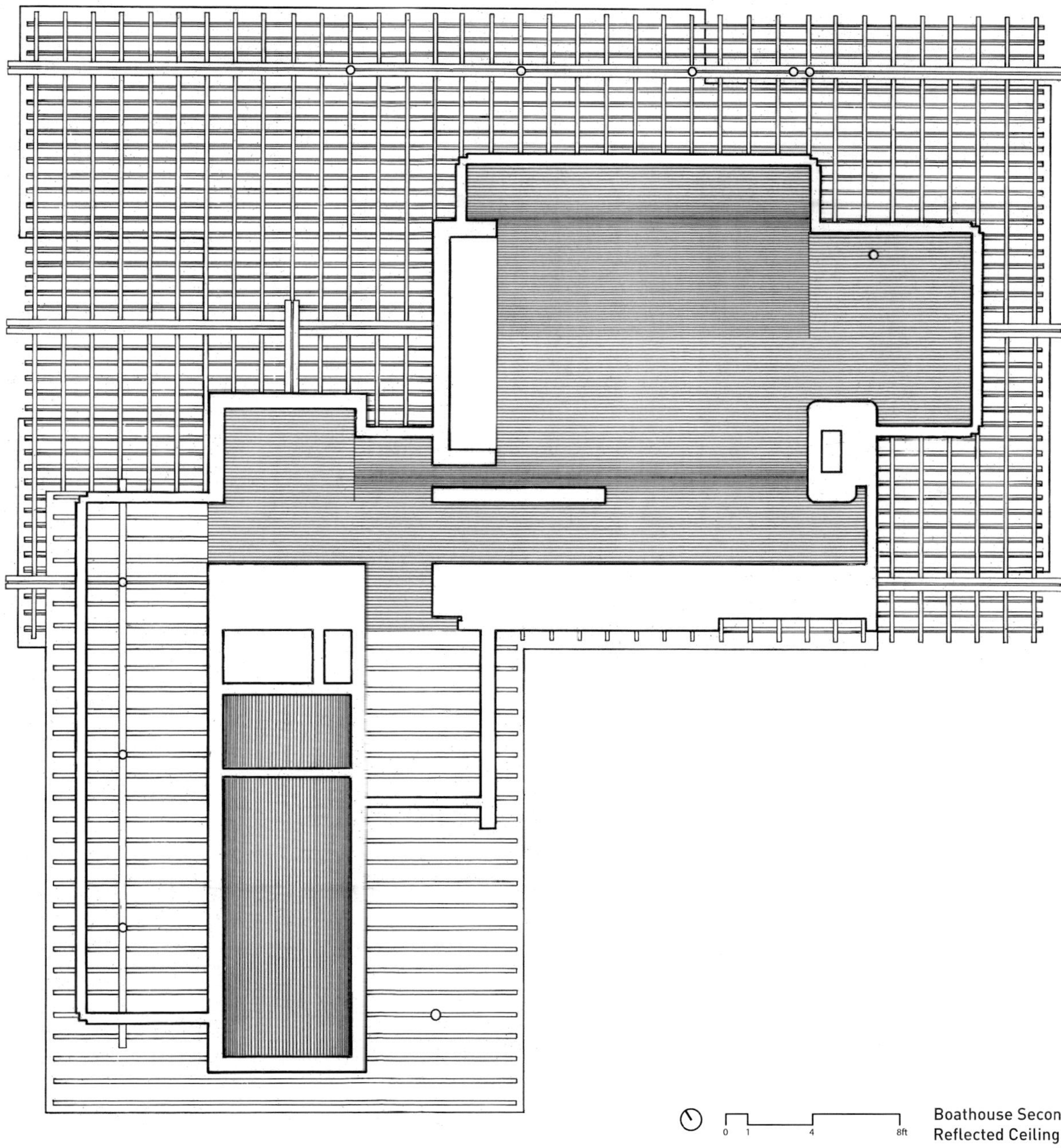



Boathouse Second Floor
Reflected Ceiling Plan

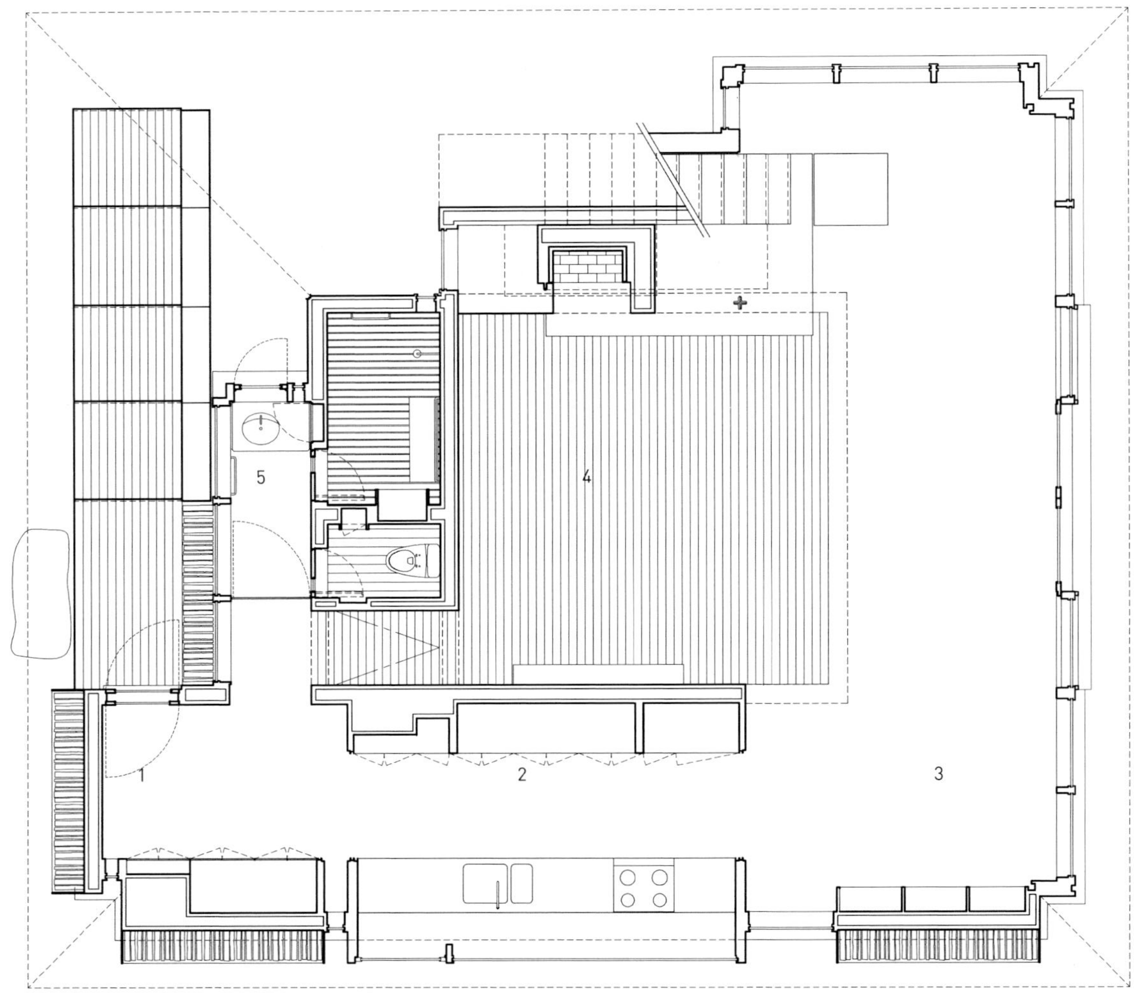


1 entry/porch
2 kitchen/porch
3 dining/porch
4 living
5 bathroom

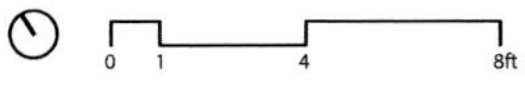


**Guest Cottage**
**Ground Floor Plan**

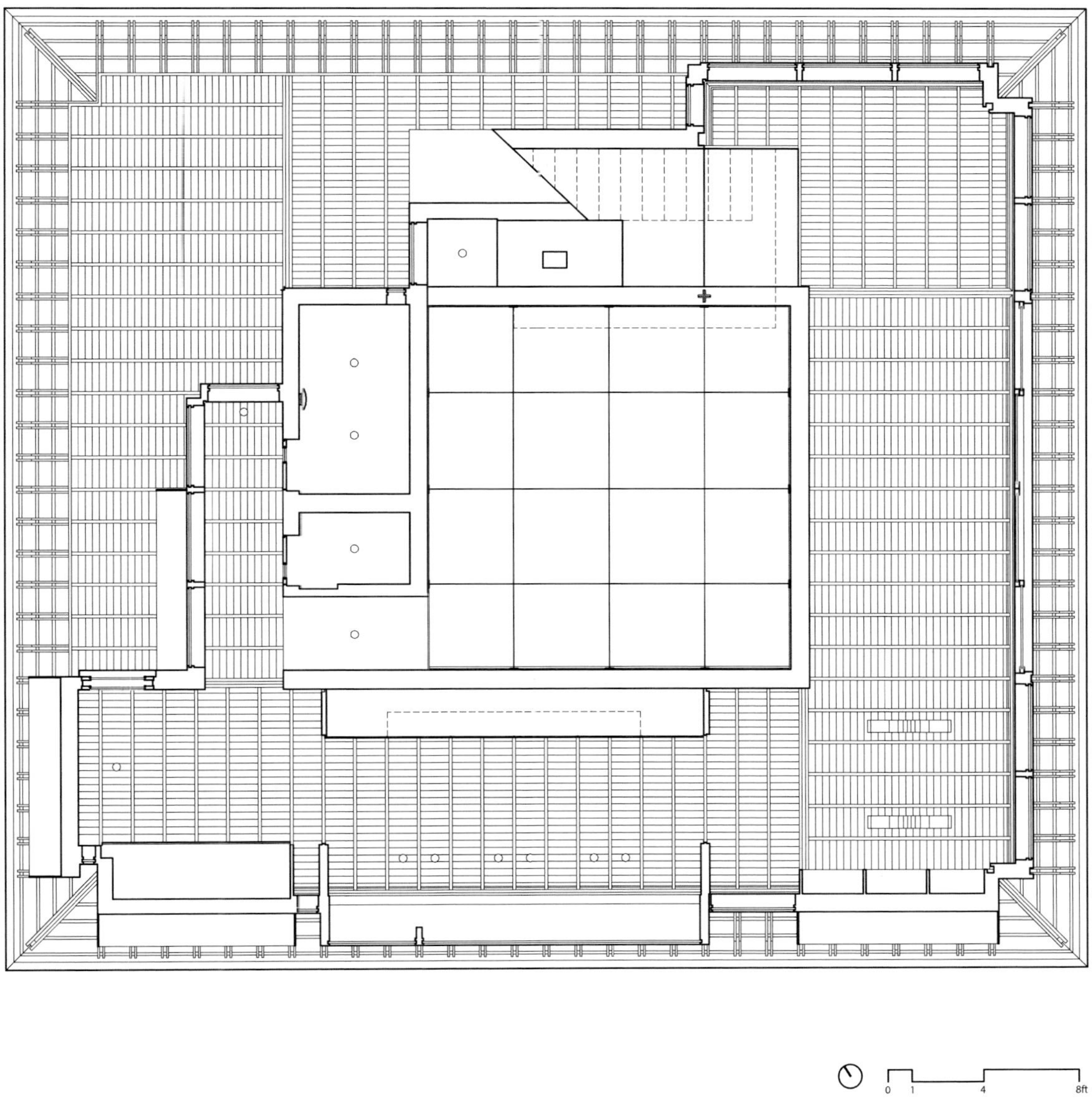


Guest Cottage Ground Floor
Reflected Ceiling Plan

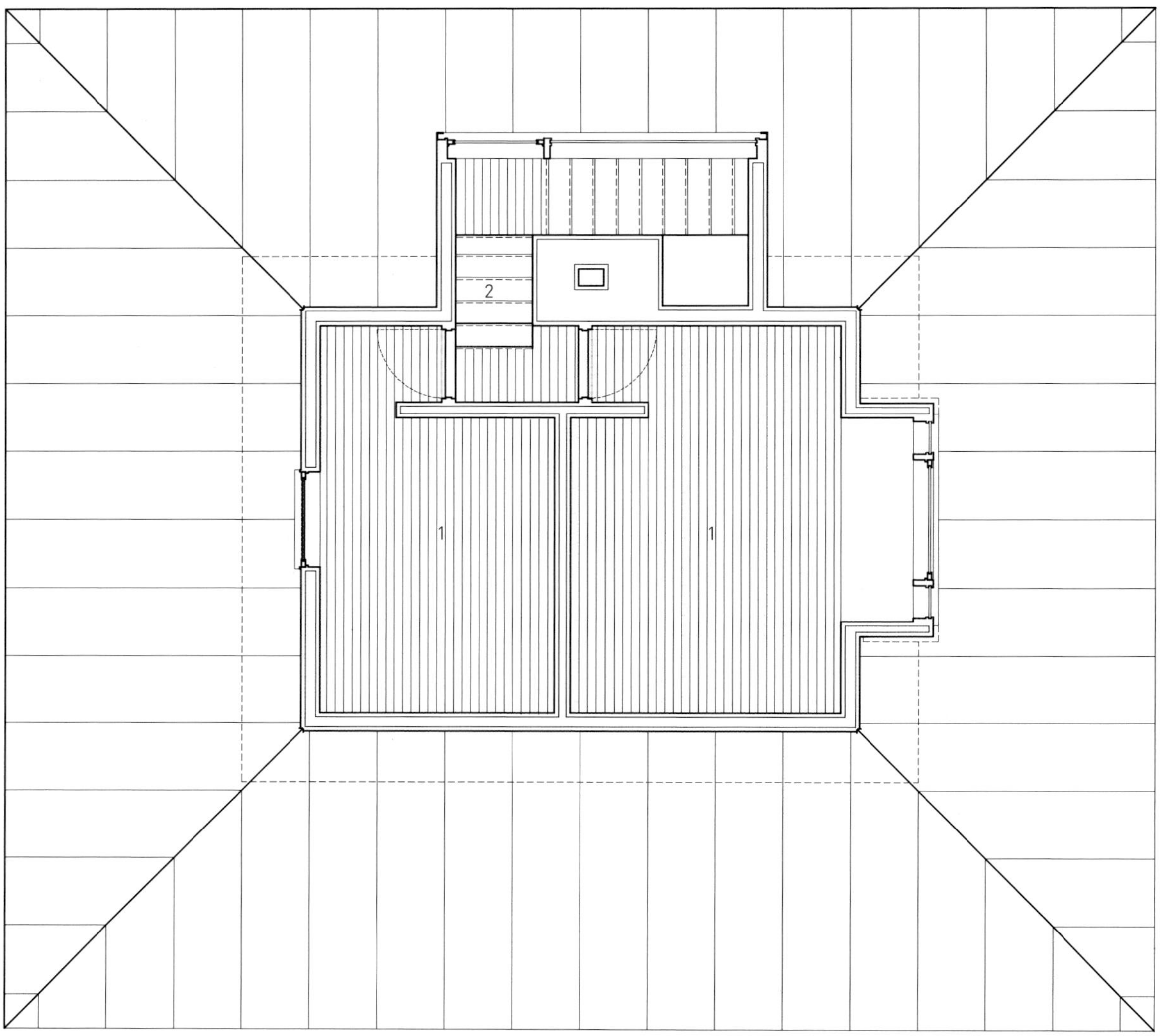


1 bedroom
2 stair down

0 1 4 8ft

**Guest Cottage**
**Second Floor**

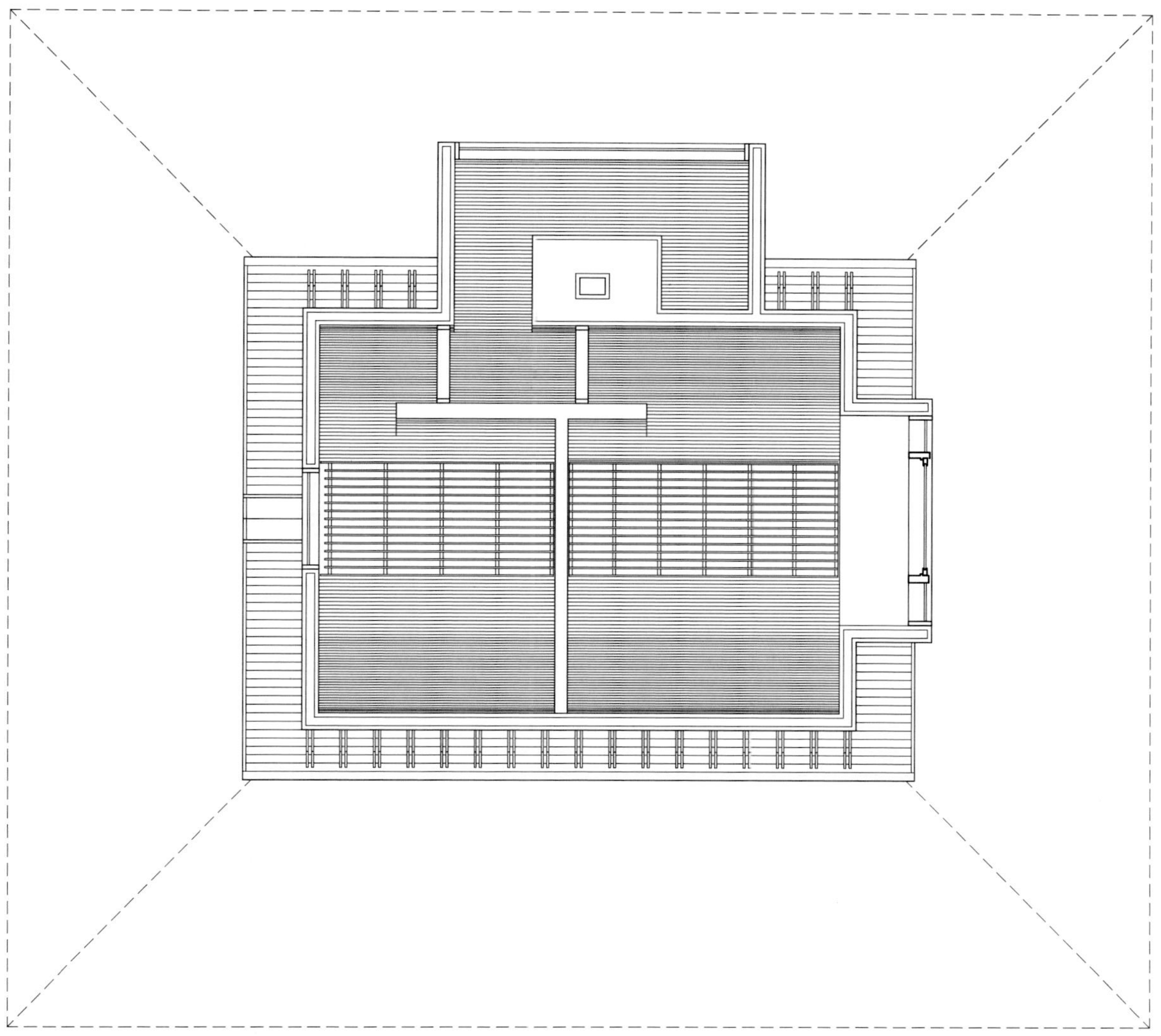

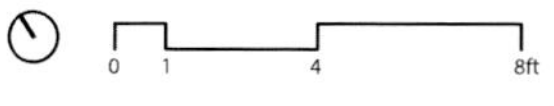


Guest Cottage Second Floor
Reflected Ceiling Plan

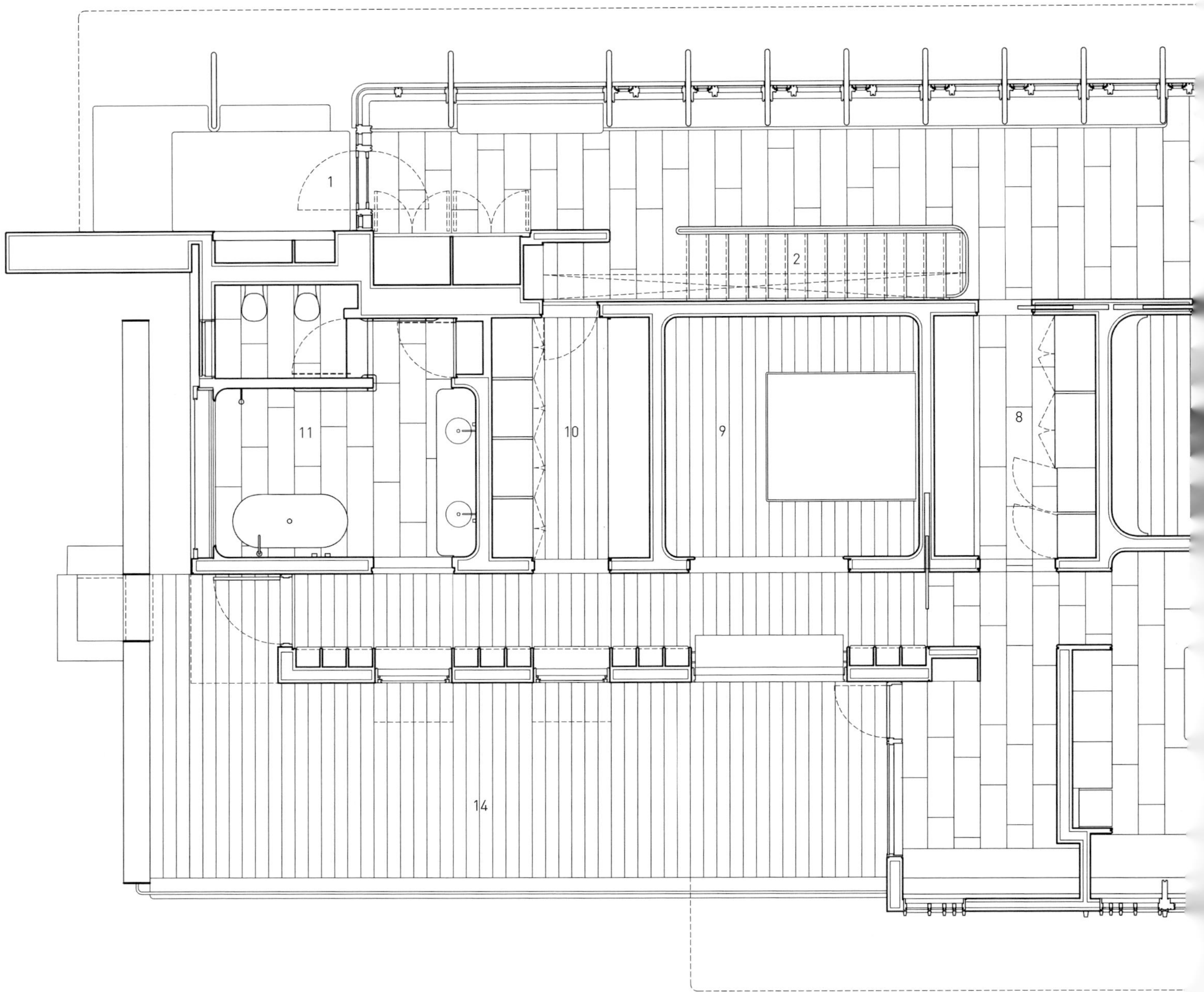

1
2
11
10
9
8
14

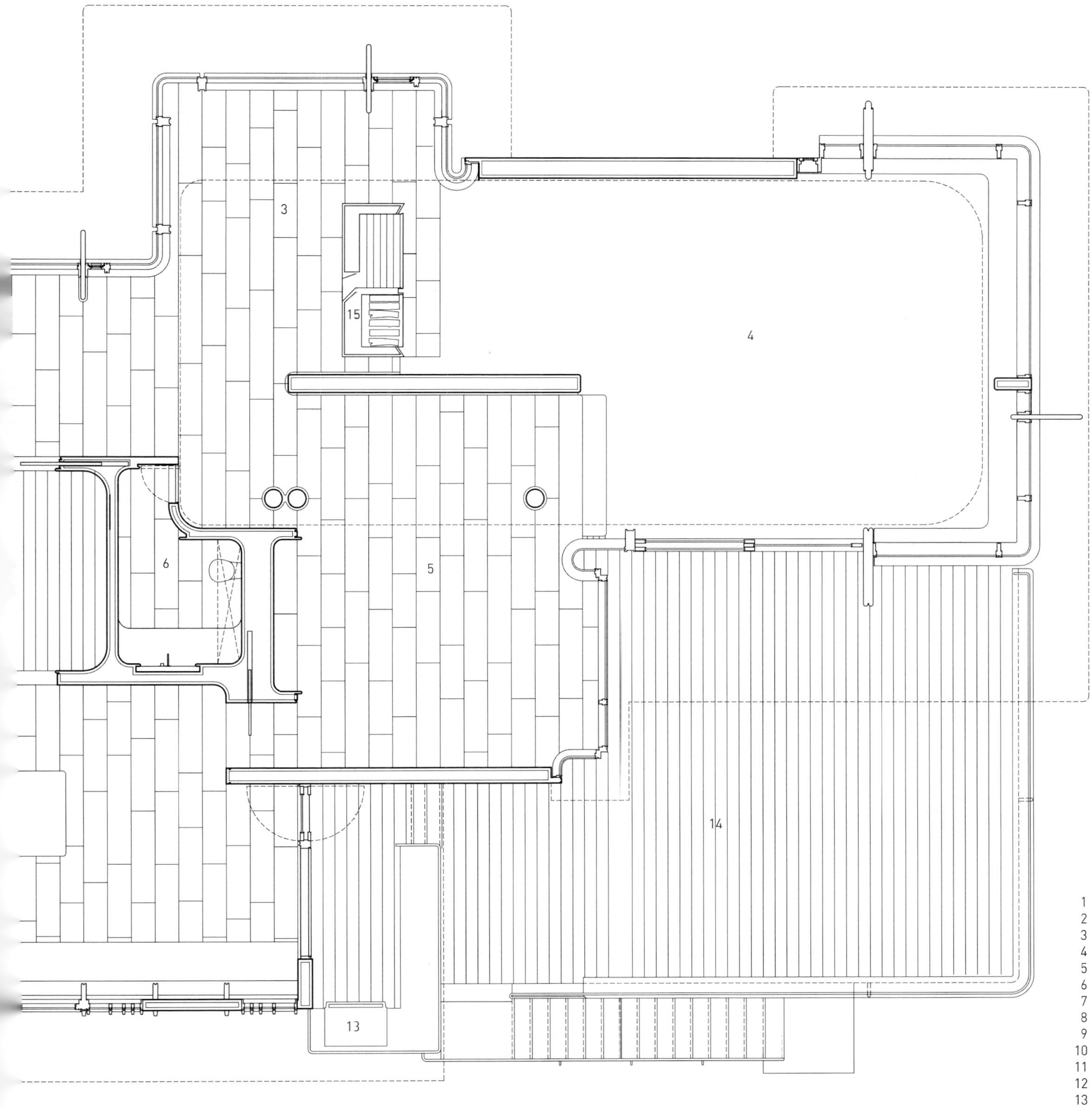


1 entry
2 stair down
3 sitting area
4 living
5 dining
6 power room
7 family room
8 pantry
9 master bedroom
10 dressing
11 master bathroom
12 kitchen
13 BBQ
14 outdoor deck
15 fireplace

**Cottage**
**Ground Floor Plan**

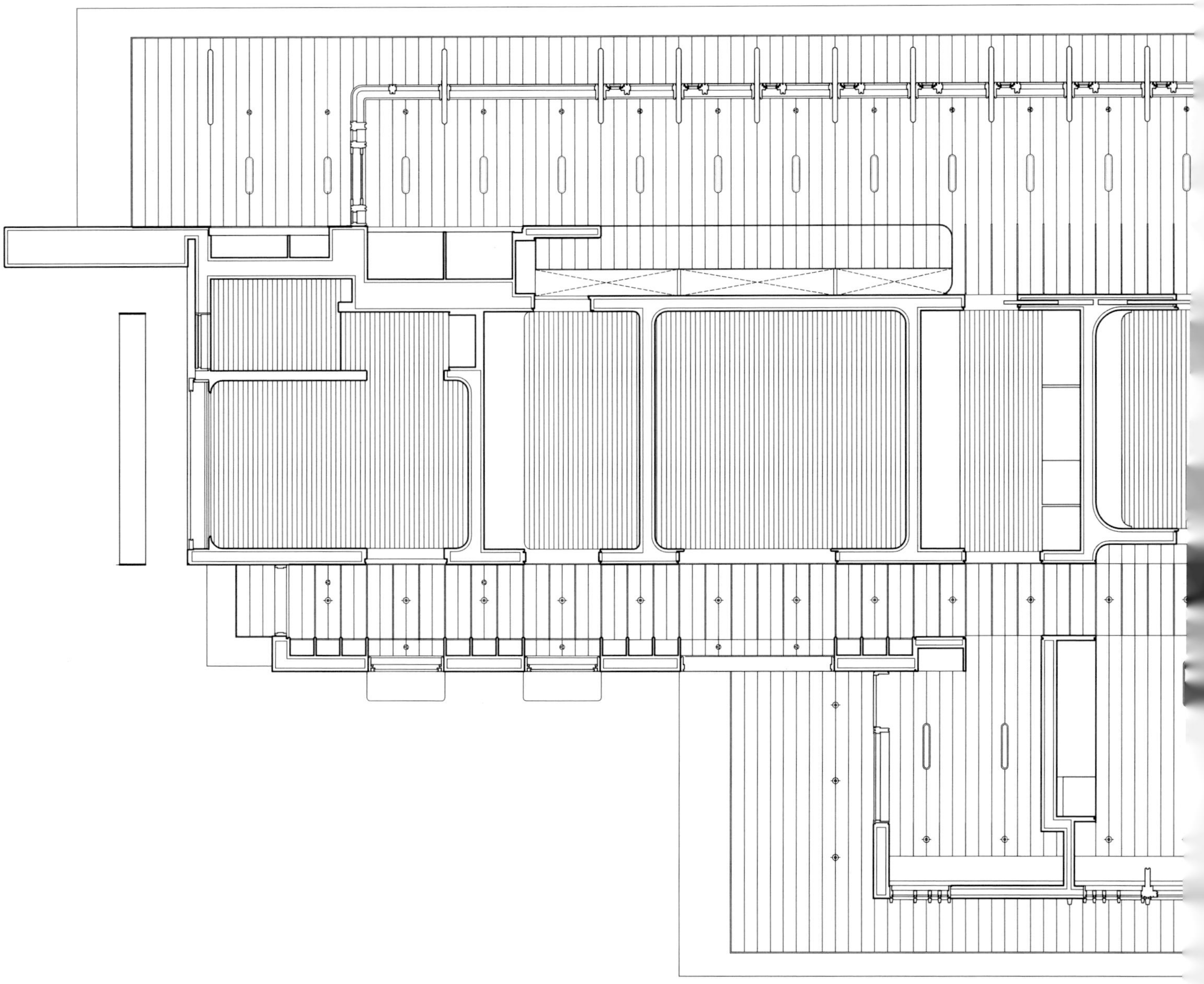

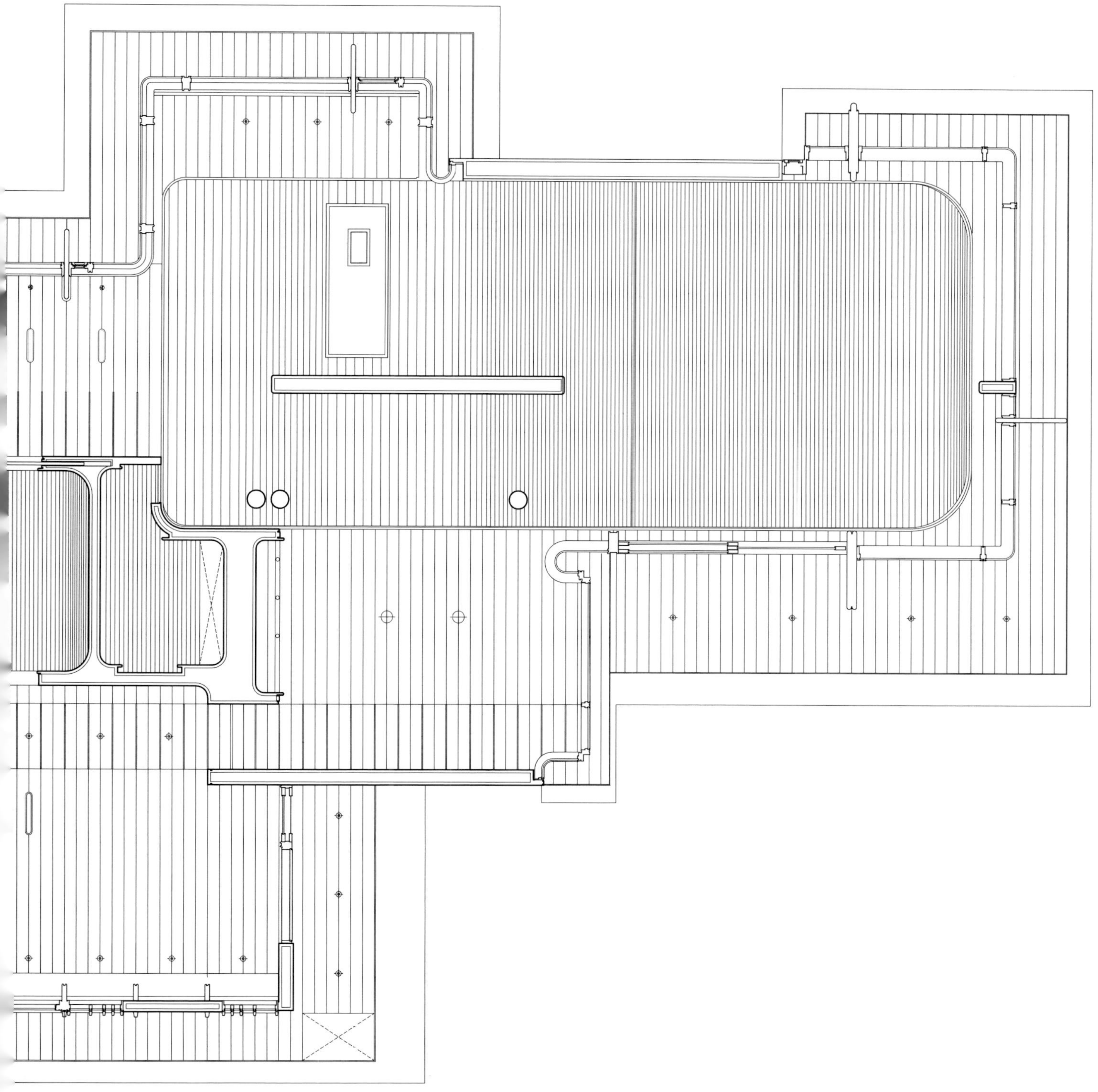

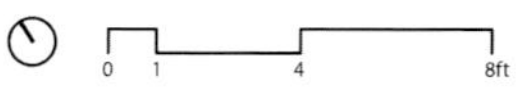


Cottage Ground Floor
Reflected Ceiling Plan

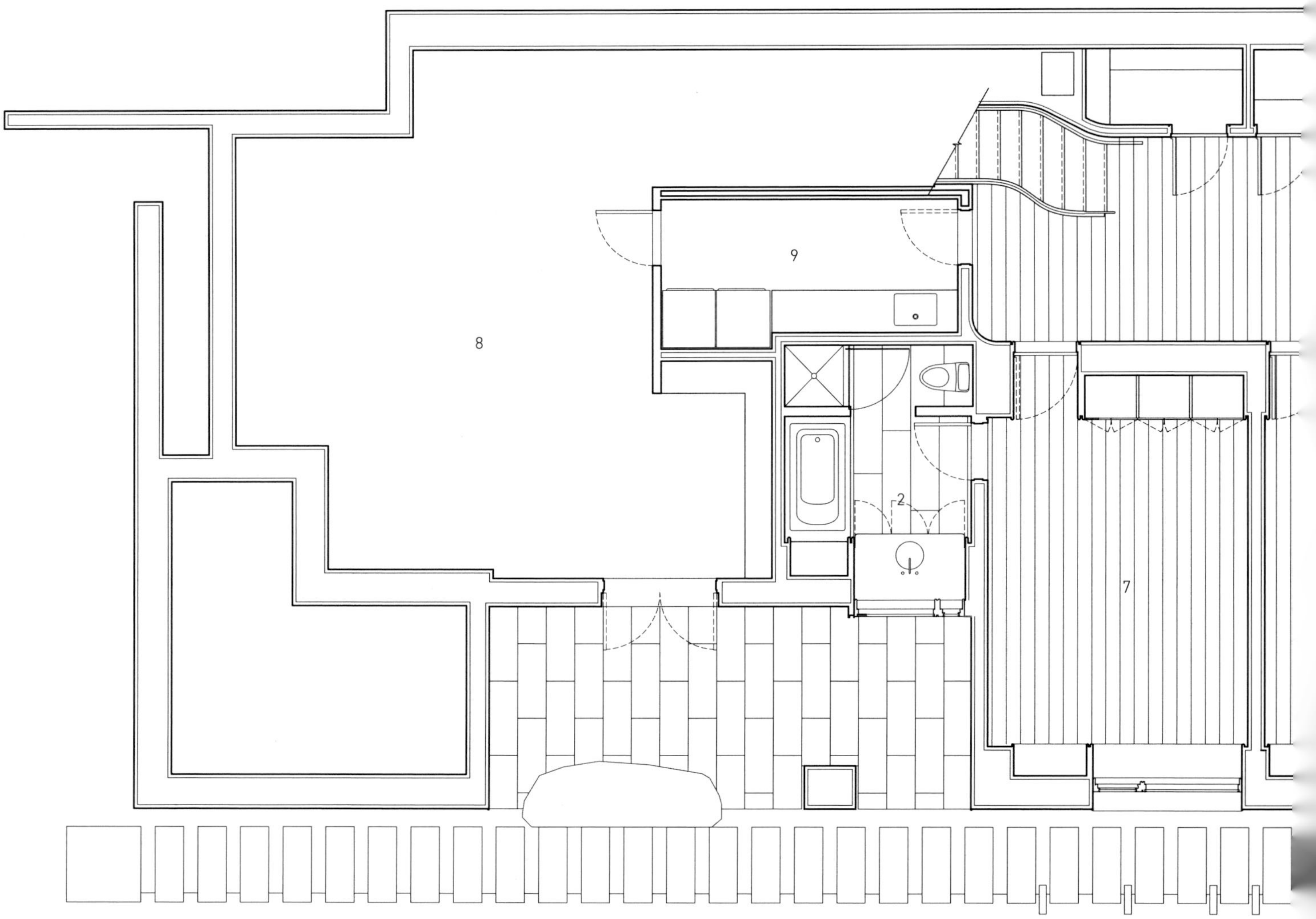

9
8
2
7

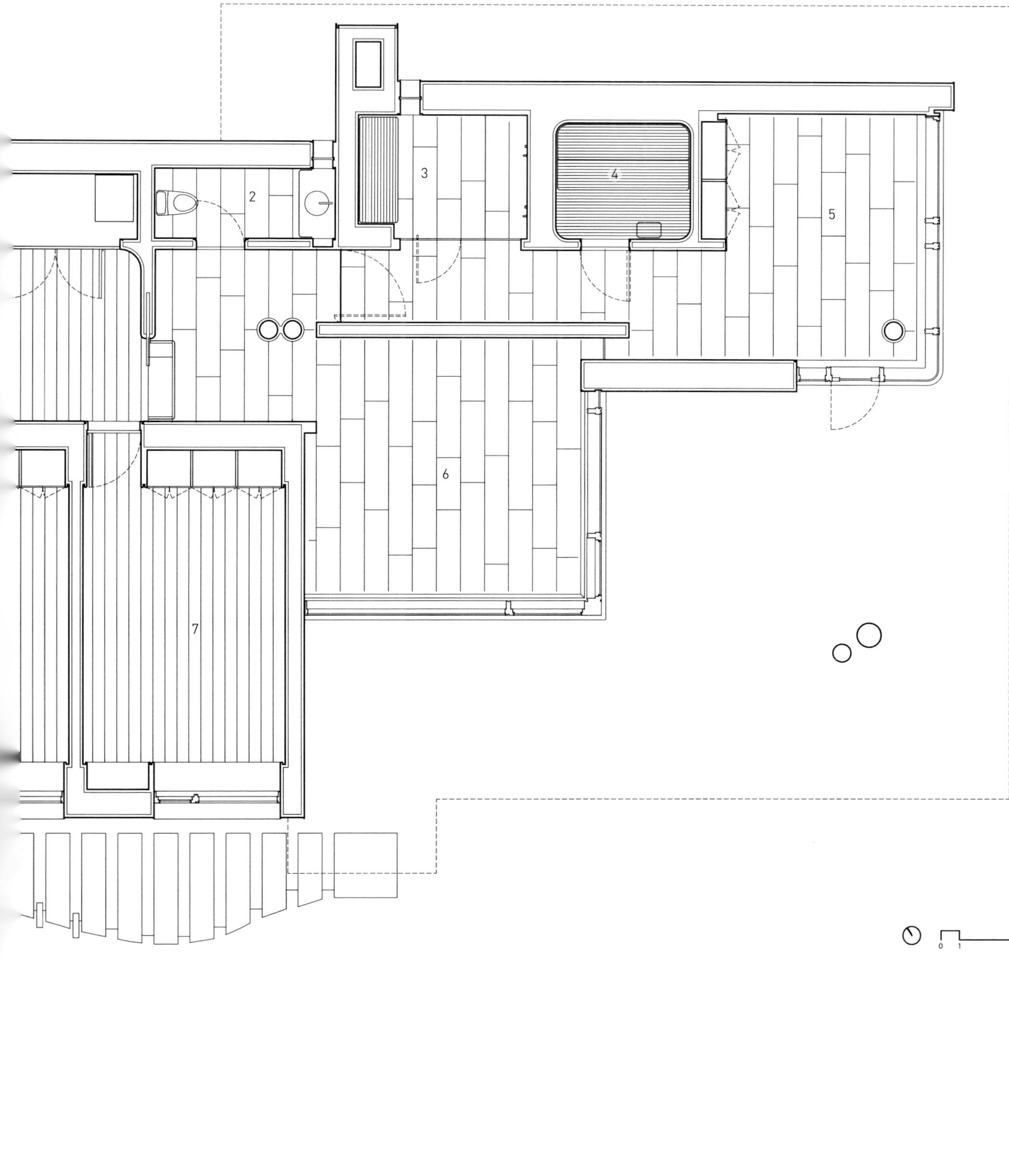


1 hall
2 bathroom
3 steam room
4 sauna
5 massage area
6 family room
7 bedroom
8 mechanical
9 laundry




**Cottage Lower Floor Plan**

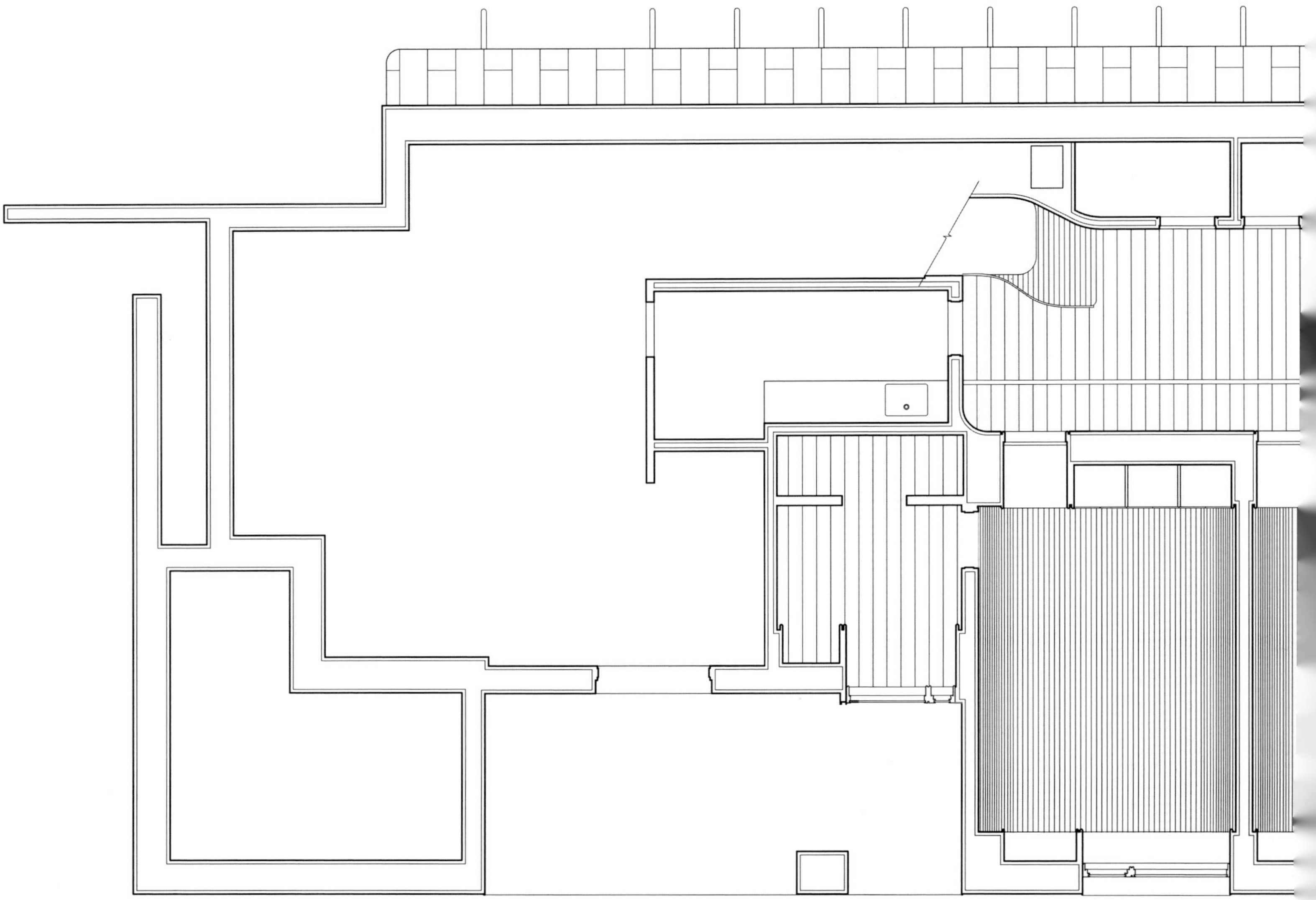

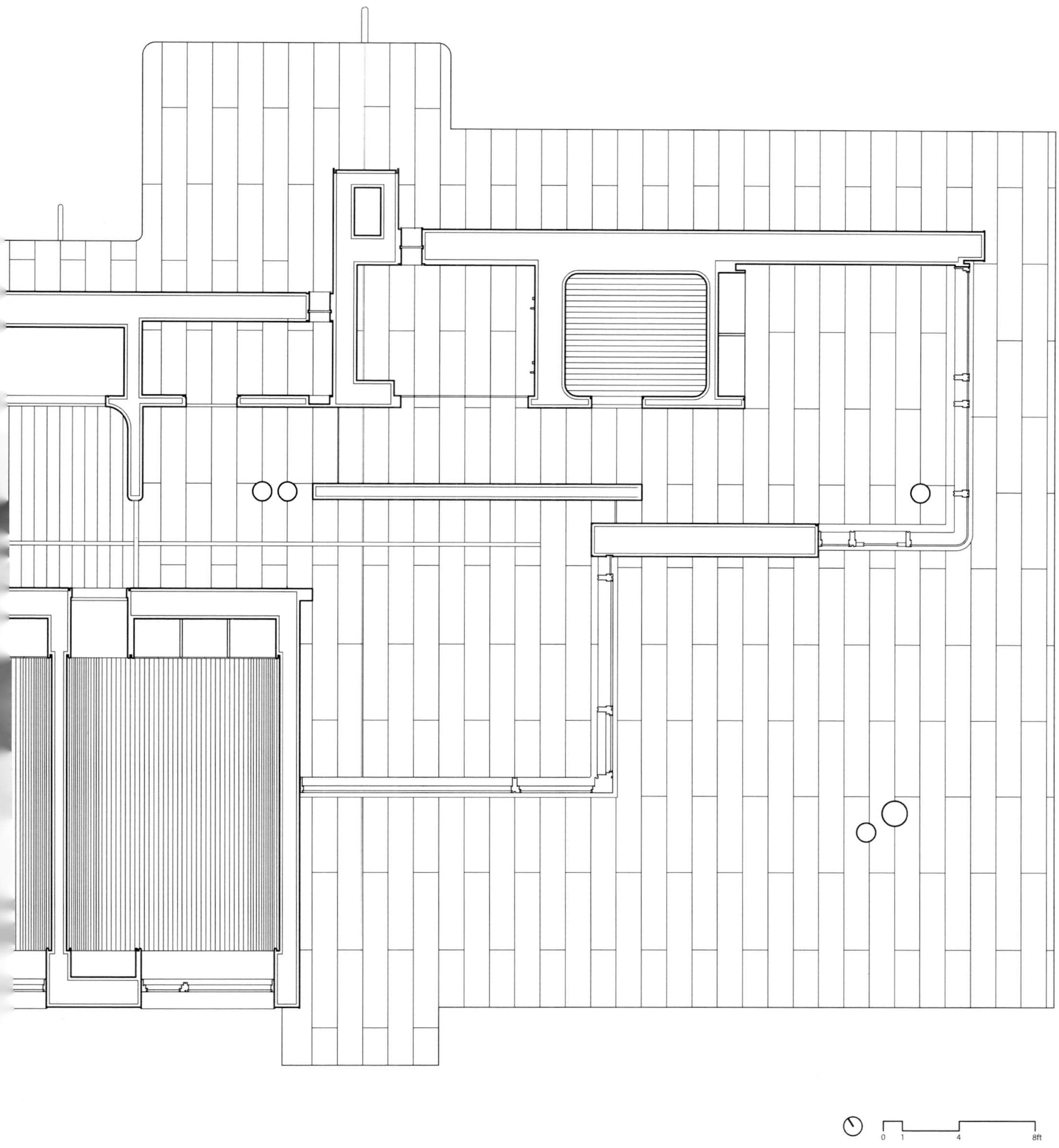


Cottage Lower Floor
Reflected Ceiling Plan

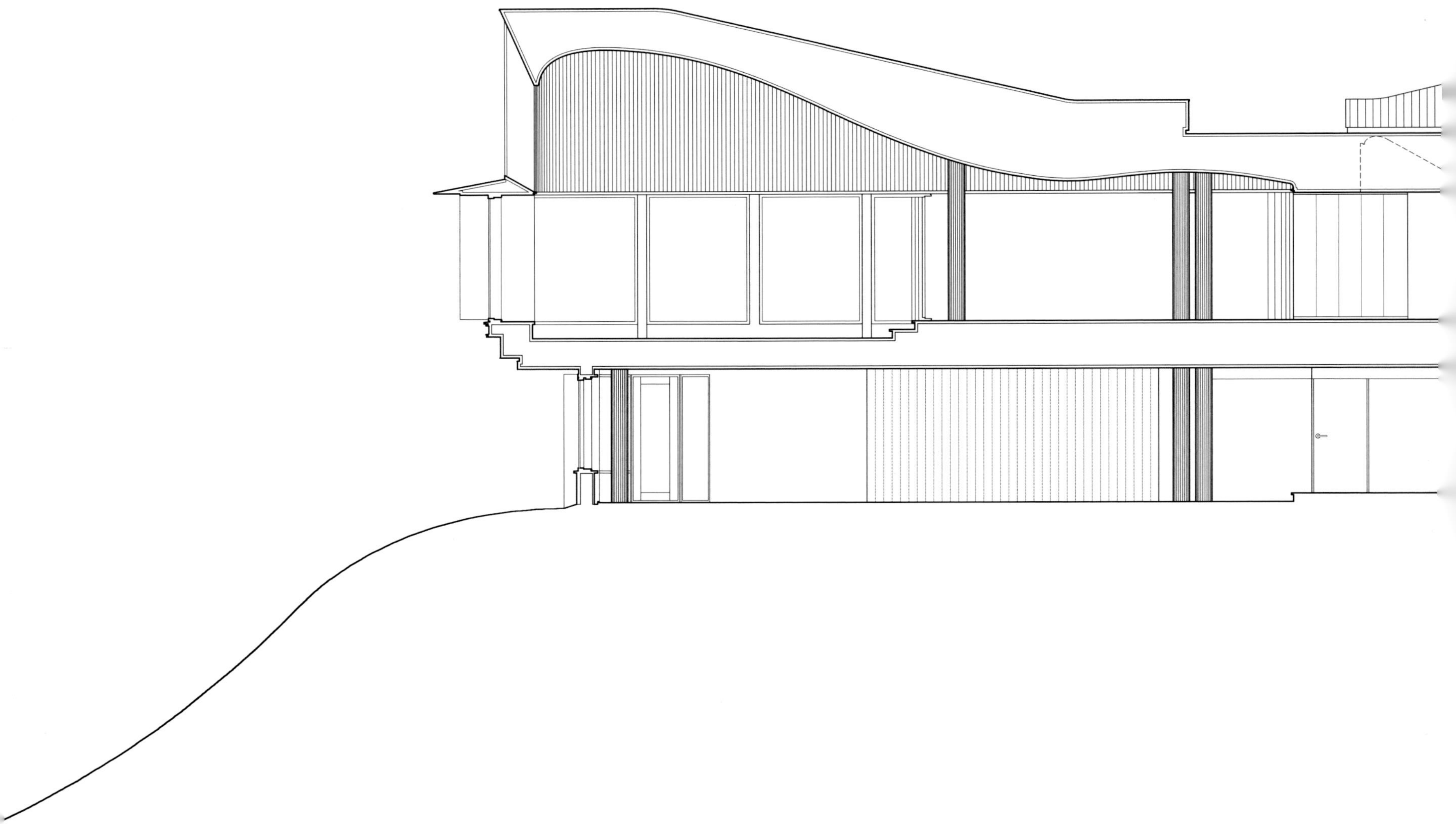

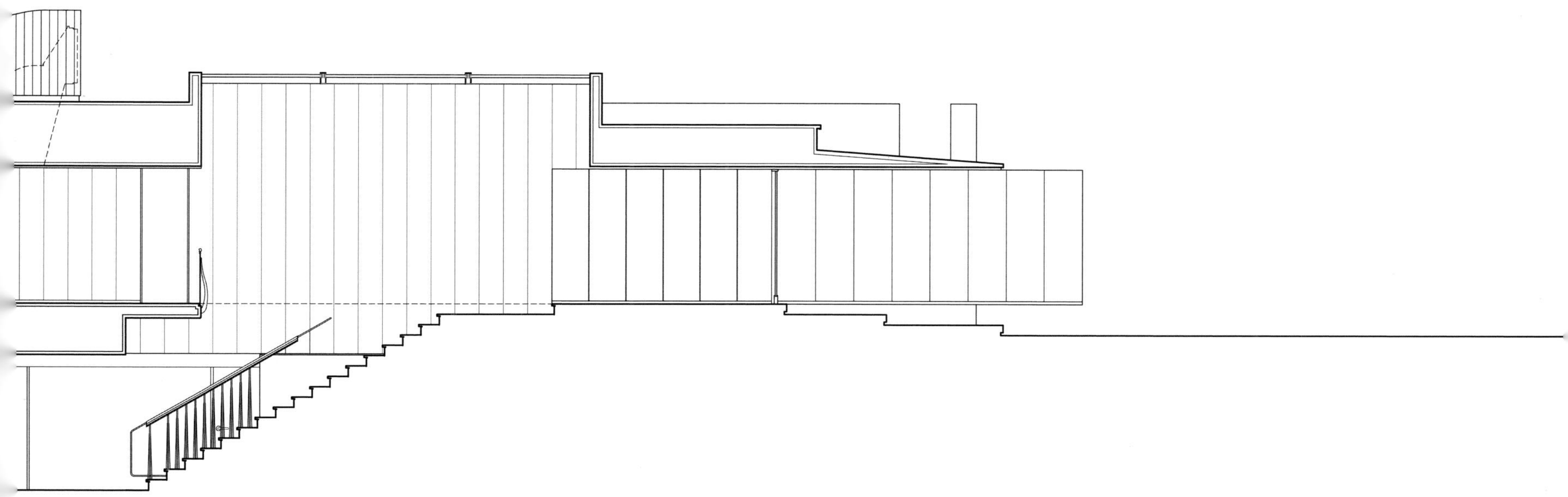

Cottage
Longitudinal Section

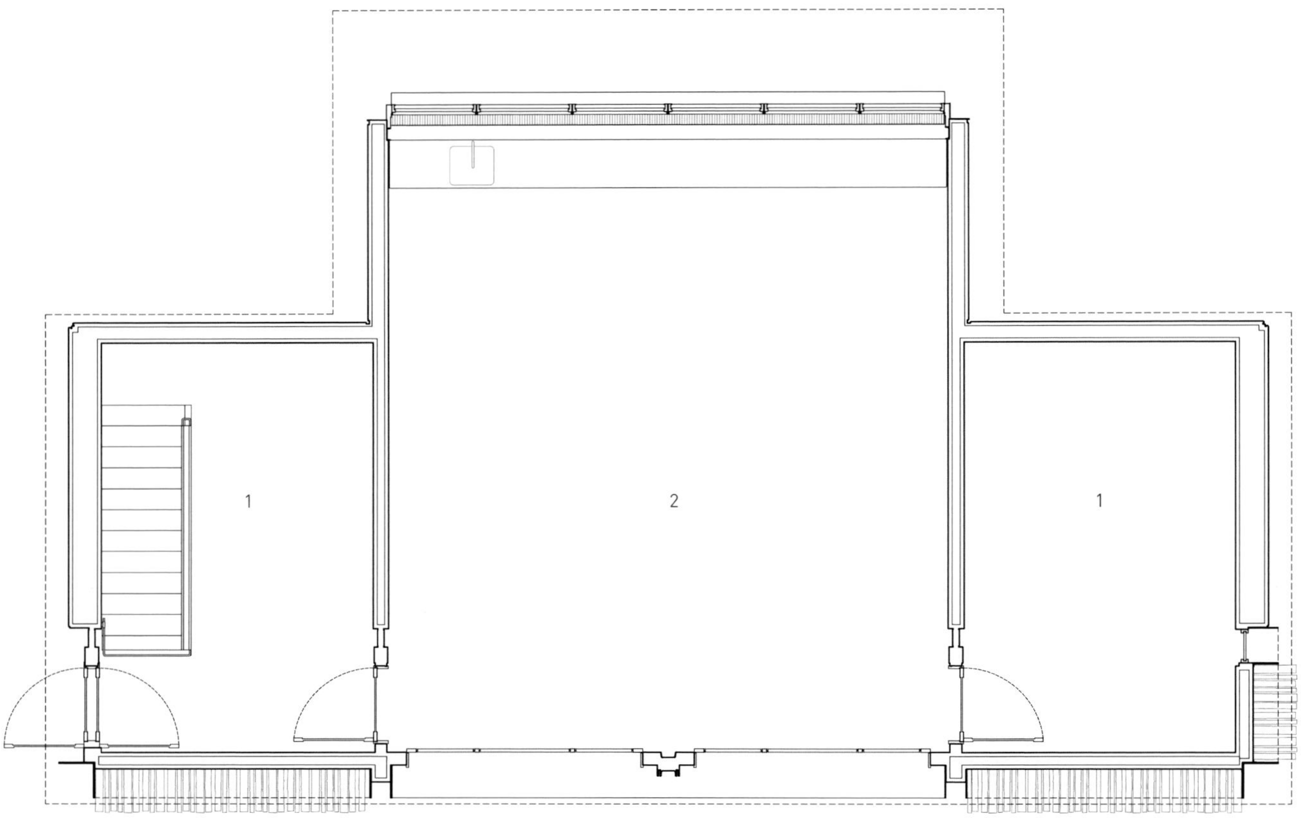


1 storage
2 garage

**Garage Floor Plan**

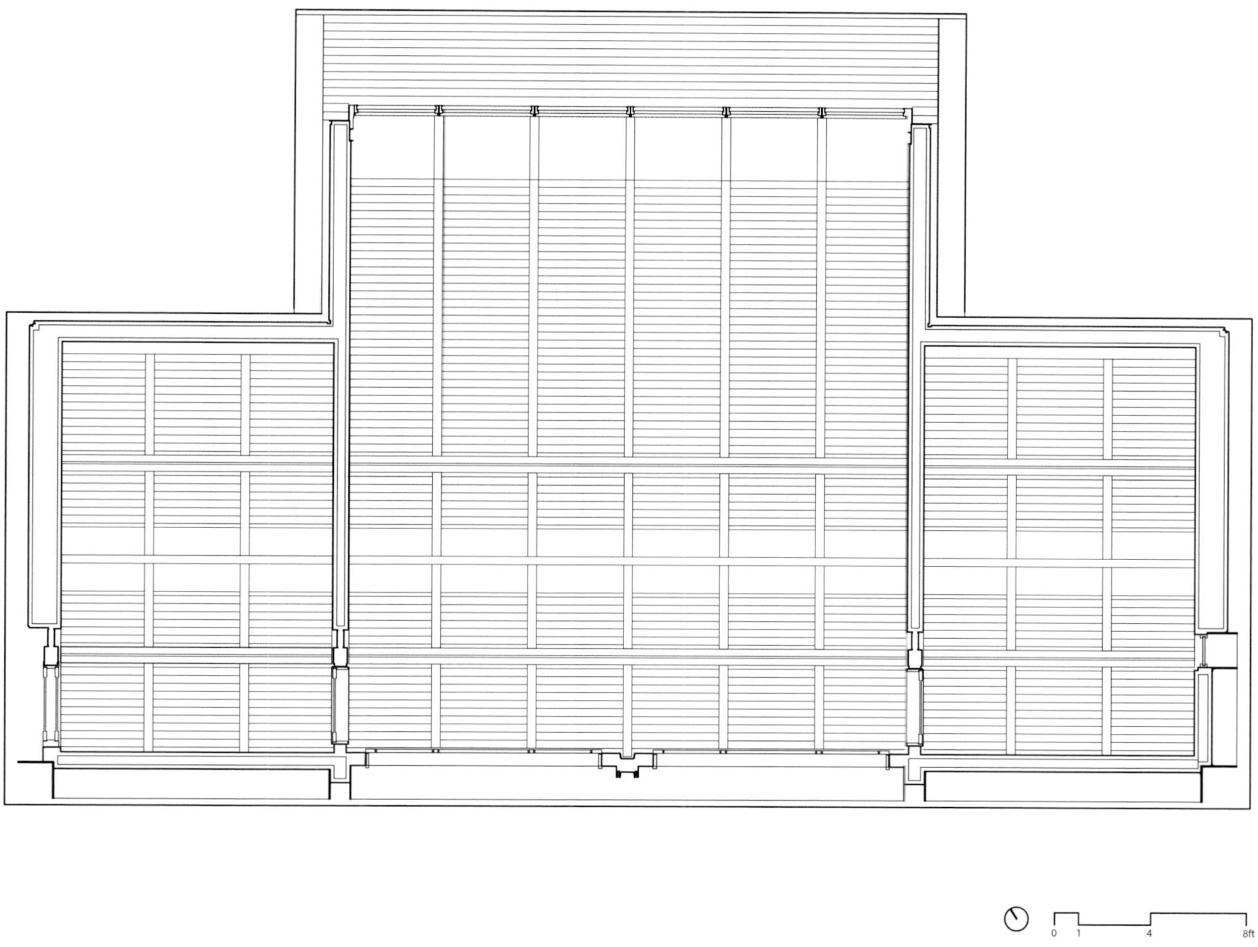

Garage
Reflected Ceiling Plan

# TIMELINE

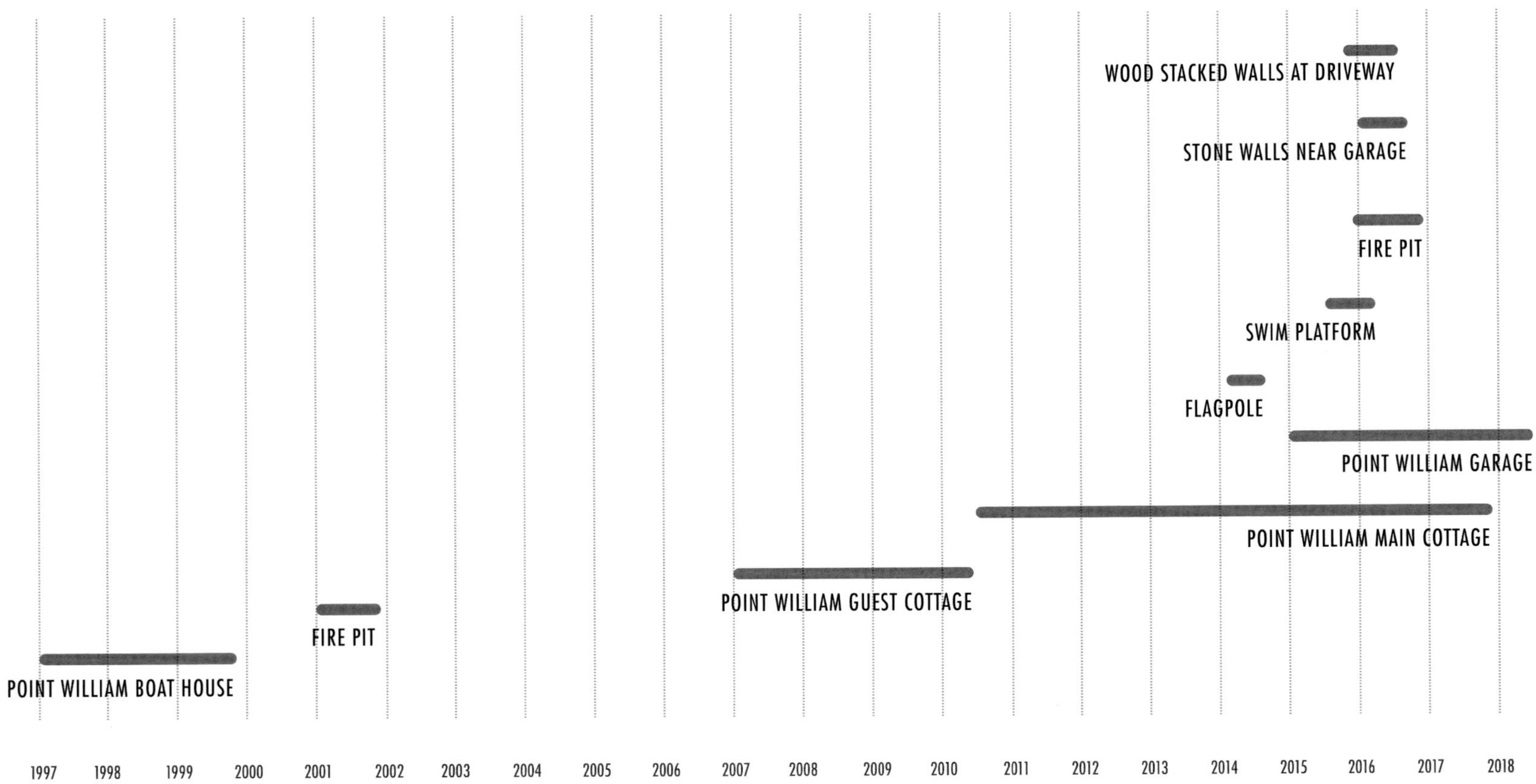
WOOD STACKED WALLS AT DRIVEWAY
STONE WALLS NEAR GARAGE
FIRE PIT
SWIM PLATFORM
FLAGPOLE
POINT WILLIAM GARAGE
POINT WILLIAM MAIN COTTAGE
POINT WILLIAM GUEST COTTAGE
FIRE PIT
POINT WILLIAM BOAT HOUSE
1997
1998
1999
2000
2001
2002
2003
2004
2005
2006
2007
2008
2009
2010
2011
2012
2013
2014
2015
2016
2017
2018

# ACKNOWLEDGMENTS

Realizing a book that captures the work of two decades of work is challenging and is only possible because of the efforts of many. Michael Webb visited the Point William site on a lovely fall day and was struck by the ensemble of built form and landscape. He recommended that this work be captured in a book. Gordon Goff at ORO agreed and this publication is a result of their enthusiasm and interest in this project. Anita Matusevics did a wonderful job as the graphic designer shaping this book. We are fortunate to work with skilled and talented photographers who are able to capture different aspects of our work and we are indebted to Edward Burtynsky, James Dow, Scott Norsworthy, and Michael Awad. Kenneth Frampton, and Michael Webb are all gifted writers who provided important insights and readings into the built work. Gerald Sheff and Shanitha Kachan are remarkable clients and the results of our journey together are embedded in this book. Finally, we would like to thank our two sons Sam and Simon for their support and enormous patience as they spent countless hours at Point William waiting for their parents.

# PROJECT TEAMS

## BOATHOUSE

Architectural Team:
Shim-Sutcliffe Architects:
Brigitte Shim and Howard Sutcliffe, with Andrew Chatham and John O'Connor (project assistants), Donald Chong and Jason-Emery Groen (presentation drawings), and James Song (model making)

Consultant Team:
Aitken + Van Groll (structural engineering); Toews Systems Design (mechanical); List Planning (planning consultant); Suzanne Powadiuk Design (lighting consultant)

Builders, Craftspeople, and Trades:
Judges Contracting: Wayne Judges (principal), Tom Montgomery (master carpenter), Takashi Sakamoto (master craftsman); Radiant City Millwork: Steve Bugler (principal)

## GUEST COTTAGE

Architectural Team:
Shim-Sutcliffe Architects:
Brigitte Shim and Howard Sutcliffe, with Andrew Kimber and Andrew Hart (project architects)

Consultant Team:
Blackwell Engineering (structural); GPY + Associates Engineering (mechanical)

Builders, Craftspeople, and Trades:
Judges Contracting: Wayne Judges (principal), Tom Montgomery (master carpenter);
J S W Manufacturing Inc: Mike du Charme, Eric Plamondon (metal fabricators); Norstar Exteriors: Mark Wilson (fabricators); Radiant City Millwork: Steve Bugler (principal)

## COTTAGE

Architectural Team:
Shim-Sutcliffe Architects:
Brigitte Shim and Howard Sutcliffe, with Stephan Leblanc and Zack Glennon (project architects)

Consultant Team:
Blackwell Engineering (structural); BK Consulting (Mechanical, Electrical); Karen Petrachenko and Chapi Chapo (interiors)

Builders, Craftspeople and Trades:
Judges Contracting: Wayne Judges (principal),Tom Montgomery (master carpenter), George Montgomery (carpenter); VMF Structures: Vic Furgiuele (builder); MCM: Gregory Rybak (principal), Oleg Izvekov, Jane Feoktistova, Richard Dubicki, Nick Savage, Witek Jasinski, Chris Plaza (Millwork); Two Degrees North: Simon Cooper, Gene Housego (millwork); Kai Leather Product Design: Kai Kruger, Rebecca Armstrong (leather); Lasertrim: Jeff Rogers (woodwork); J S W Manufacturing Inc: Mike du Charme, Eric Plamondon, Matt Nicholson (metal fabricators); Mariani Metals: Vince Mariani, Florin Novac (metal fabricators); Norstar Exteriors: Mark Wilson (fabricators); CB Marble: Armi Leonetti (stonework); Tradewood Industries: David Tausenfreund, Marcel Mulder (custom windows and doors); Leal Construction: Dan Leal (concrete), Concord Construction: Mark Weiner (concrete); Bulthaup: Stefan Sybydlo (kitchen); Canadian Building Hardware: James Alati (hardware); Upper Canada Hardware: Mike Ormonde (hardware); Anony Lighting: Christian Lo, David Ryan (lighting); Dark Tools: Glen Boccini (LED lighting); Nelson Garrett: Chris Nelson (Custom Lighting); Mirabelli HVAC: Pat Mirabelli (mechanical); Morrow: Stephen Robinson (electric); Boone Plumbing: Steve Boone (plumbing); Entertaining Interiors: Rob Patterson, Bill Dobbs (home automation); Brackenrig Landscaping: Rick Wright, Jaymie Brasi, Zoe Grubb, Steve, Sereda, Logan Harrison, Theo Robert, Ben Tebo, Jason Basso, Dale Antcliffe (landscaping); Vita Roof, Joy Schmidt (green roof)

## GARAGE

Architectural Team:
Shim-Sutcliffe Architects:
Brigitte Shim and Howard Sutcliffe, with Zack Glennon (project architect)

Consultant Team:
Engineering Link Inc. (structural)

Builders, Craftspeople, and Trades:
Judges Contracting: Wayne Judges (principal), Tom Montgomery (master carpenter), George Montgomery (carpenter); MCM: Gregory Rybak (principal), Oleg Izvekov, Jane Feoktistova, Richard Dubicki, Nick Savage, Witek Jasinski, Chris Plaza (millwork); J S W Manufacturing Inc: Mike du Charme, Eric Plamondon, Matt Nicholson (metal fabricators); Norstar Exteriors: Mark Wilson (fabricators); Canadian Building Hardware: James Alati (hardware); Upper Canada Hardware: Mike Ormonde (hardware); Mirabelli HVAC: Pat Mirabelli (mechanical), Morrow: Stephen Robinson (electric); Boone Plumbing: Steve Boone (plumbing); Two Degrees North: Simon Cooper, Gene Housego (millwork); Tradewood Industries: David Tausenfreund, Marcel Mulder (custom windows and doors); Torp Inc: Arne Nordtorp (Windows), Thompson's Glass: Wes Thompson (glazing); Leal Construction: Dan Leal (concrete), Concord Construction: Mark Weiner (concrete); Entertaining Interiors: Rob Patterson, Bill Dobbs (home automation)

# AWARDS AND PUBLICATIONS

## Point William Boat House

AWARDS

2004
Royal Architectural Institute of Canada (RAIC), Governor General Medal for Architecture: Muskoka Boathouse, Lake Muskoka, Ontario

2001
North American Wood Award Program, Wood Design Award of Honor: Muskoka Boathouse, Lake Muskoka, Ontario

1999
Progressive Architecture Citation: Muskoka Boathouse, Lake Muskoka, Ontario

PUBLICATIONS

2010
Mornement, Adam. *Boathouses.* London: Frances-Lincoln Limited, 2010: 132-137.

2005
Bouknight, Joanne Keller. *Celebrating the American Home: 50 Great Houses from 50 American Architects.* Newtown, CT: Taunton Press, 2005: 140-143.

2004
Adamczyk, Georges. *Maisons-lieux / Houses-Places. Architecture contemporaire au Canada / Contemporary Canadian Architecture.* Montréal: Centre international d'art contemporain de Montréa, 2005: 61-68, 131-140. 177-184.

2003
Carter, Brian, and Annette LeCuyer, eds. *Off the Radar.* Architectural Design. vol. 73, no.1. Chichester: Wiley-Academy, 2003: 70-74.

Knight, Robert W. *A House on the Water: Inspirations for Living at the Water's Edge.* Newtown, CT: The Taunton Press, 2003: 132-139.

2002
Cramer, James P., and Jennifer Evans Yankopolus, eds. *Almanac of Architecture & Design, Third Edition.* Atlanta, GA: Greenway Communications, 2002: 183.

Davis, Jodie, and Diane Strong, eds., *100 of the World's Best Houses.* Melbourne: The Images Publishing Group Pty Ltd. 2002: 226-229.

2001
Barreneche, Raul and Cathy Lang Ho. House: *American Houses for the New Century.* New York: Universe Press. 2001: 36-44.

de Visser, John and Judy Ross. *Shelter at the Shore: The Boathouses of Muskoka Ontario.* Erin: Boston Mills Press, 2001: 95-99.

Gillmor, Don, "On the Waterfront." *Saturday Night Magazine* (May 2001): 45-51.

Omata, Naho. "Shim-Sutcliffe Architects: Muskoka Boathouse, Moorelands Camp Dining Hall." *a+u Architecture and Urbanism,* Feature: Wooden Architecture no. 366 (March 2001): 56-69.

"The Wood Design Awards 2001." *Wood Design and Building.* no. 17 (Autumn 2001): 19-21.

"The Wood Design Awards 2001." Wood | Holz | Bois, no. 35 (Autumn 2001): 10-11.

Zeng, Lian. "New Architecture in Canada - Selected Works." *World Architecture: New Architecture in Canada.* Sponsored by Tsinghua University and the Bejing Research Institute of Architectural Design. Bejing World Architecture Magazine Publication, vol 136, no. 10 (2001): 68-73.

2000
Barreneche, Raul A. "Muskoka Boathouse, Shim Sutcliffe Architects." *Architecture Magazine,* vol. 89, no. 10, (October 2000): 92-99.

Rasch, Horst, "Heimathafen. Hause." *Arkitekur, Design, Kunst, Garten, Reise.* February 2000: 128-133.

1999
46th Annual P/A Awards, "Muskoka Boathouse - Shim-Sutcliffe Architects." *Architecture Magazine,* vol. 88, no. 4: 94-95.

**ORO Editions**
Publishers of Architecture, Art, and Design
Gordon Goff: Publisher

www.oroeditions.com
info@oroeditions.com

Published by ORO Editions



Text by Kenneth Frampton and Michael Webb
Book Design by Anita Matusevics, Wonder Incorporated
Pre Press: Type A Print Inc., Canada
Managing Editor: Jake Anderson
Copy Editor: Sarah Brohman

10 9 8 7 6 5 4 3 2 1 First Edition

ISBN: 978-1-943532-54-4

Color Separations and Printing:
ORO Group Ltd.
Printed in China.

ORO Editions makes a continuous effort to minimize the overall carbon footprint of its publications. As part of this goal, ORO Editions, in association with Global ReLeaf, arranges to plant trees to replace those used in the manufacturing of the paper produced for its books. Global ReLeaf is an international campaign run by American Forests, one of the world's oldest nonprofit conservation organizations. Global ReLeaf is American Forests' education and action program that helps individuals, organizations, agencies, and corporations improve the local and global environment by planting and caring for trees.

# IMAGE CREDITS

IMAGE CREDITS

The architects and publisher have made every effort to identify ownership in the use of images and copyrighted material. In the event of an inadvertent omission or error, please notify the publisher.

PHOTOGRAPHY CREDITS

Michael Awad: 60, 61, 62

Ed Burtynsky: 8-9, 18-19, 23, 30, 32, 33, 43, 44-45, 46-47, 57, 91, 96-97, 163, 172-173, 177

James Dow: 29, 31, 63, 67, 68-69, 73, 75, 76, 77, 79, 81, 82, 84, 102-103, 104-105, 109, 112, 113, 116-117, 196

Anita Matusevics: 241

Scott Norsworthy: 34, 35, 37, 39, 42, 48-49, 50-51, 71, 83, 86-87, 92-93, 94-95, 98, 99, 118-119, 122, 125, 126-127, 128-129, 131, 133, 137,1 38-139, 140-141, 142, 144, 145, 146, 148, 149, 150, 151, 153, 155, 156, 157, 159, 160, 166, 167, 169, 170, 171, 174, 176, 178, 179, 181, 183, 185, 186, 187, 189, 191, 193, 194, 195, 201

Brigitte Shim: 3, 5, 89, 147

Howard Sutcliffe: 7, 59, 65, 66

Simon Sutcliffe: 120-121, 52-53

DRAWING CREDITS

Derived from Geology of Ontario map of the western Superior Province (Ontario Geological Survey, 1991): 2

Jeanie Lim: 3

Archives of Ontario, Map and Chart of the Muskoka Lakes, Tourist and canoeist index, 1899. Created by G.W. Marshall. C 60, I0030832, F006164/Map and Chart of the Muskoka Lakes: Tourist and canoeist index,1899/Copyright Public Domain, Copyright expired: 6

Christine Boyer: 24 upper

Zack Glennon: 198, 199

Kenneth Frampton sketchbook: 20, 21, 24, 28, 30, 32, 34, 40, 41

Andrew Kimber: 115, 218, 219

Stephane LeBlanc: 123, 130, 134, 168

Jeanie Lim: 4

Howard Sutcliffe: 10, 11, 25, 26, 27, 55, 58, 61, 64, 66, 71, 72, 74, 80, 85, 100, 101, 108, 114, 115, 132, 154, 158, 161, 162, 165, 168, 178, 180, 183, 184, 188, 192, 197, 198, 199, 202, 203, 204, 206, 207, 208, 210, 211, 212, 213

Donald Chong, Jason Emory Groen: 78, 214, 215, 216, 217

Ryan Beecroft, Arya Tahvili: 24, 220, 221, 223, 225, 227, 229, 231, 232, 233.

Cover of *Vers Une Architecture* by Le Corbusier, from Kenneth Frampton's library: 22

Auguste Choisy, 1899. *Histoire de l'architecture*. p. 415 vol. 1: 23

MODEL CREDITS

James Song: 60, 61, 62

FROM THE ARCHIVES

Canadian Centre for Architecture

Printed from a photomechanical transfer or photograph; original model or drawing in the collection of the Centre Canadien d'Architecture / Canadian Centre for Architecture, Montréal. © Shim-Sutcliffe Architects.

Models: 60, 61, 62

Drawings: 26, 27, 55, 58, 61, 64, 66, 70, 72, 74, 78, 80, 85, 100, 101, 108, 114, 123, 130, 132, 134, 154, 158, 161, 162, 164, 165, 168, 178, 180, 183, 184, 188, 214, 215, 216, 217

DRAWINGS IN OPENING TITLE SEQUENCE

Geological Map: Derived from Geology of Ontario map of the western Superior Province (Ontario Geological Survey 1991).

Wood Milling Lumber Cuts: Riven and quarter sawn lumber producing stable vertical end grain from logs.

Map and Chart of the Muskoka Lakes: Tourist and canoeist index, 1899
Published by G.W. Marshall, Toronto
Reference Code: C 60
Archives of Ontario, I0030832

# CONTRIBUTORS

## SHIM-SUTCLIFFE ARCHITECTS

**Brigitte Shim and A. Howard Sutcliffe** are principals in the design firm Shim-Sutcliffe Architects. Shim-Sutcliffe's built work explores the integration and interrelated scales of architecture, landscape, and furniture and fittings. To date, Shim and Sutcliffe have received fifteen Governor General's Medals and Awards for Architecture from the Royal Architectural Institute of Canada and an American Institute of Architects National Honor Award along with many other professional accolades for their built work ranging from projects for non-profit groups to public and private clients. Their work has been published internationally and they have both lectured around the world sharing interest and passion for design at all scales. Brigitte Shim is also a professor at the John H. Daniels Faculty of Architecture, Landscape and Design at the University of Toronto. Brigitte Shim and A. Howard Sutcliffe are Fellows of the Royal Architectural Institute of Canada (FRAIC), Honorary Fellows of the American Institute of Architects (Hon. FAIA), and elected member of the Royal Canadian Academy (RCA). In January 2013, Brigitte Shim and A. Howard Sutcliffe were both awarded the Order of Canada, "for their contributions as architects designing sophisticated structures that represent the best of Canadian design to the world."

## PHOTOGRAPHY

**Ed Burtynsky** is a photographer based in Toronto known for his large format photographs of industrial landscapes. His work is housed in more than fifty museums including the Guggenheim Museum in New York, the National Gallery of Canada in Ottawa, and the Bibliothèque nationale de France in Paris. Ed Burtynsky was commissioned by *Architecture Magazine* to shoot the Point William Boathouse in 2000. Ed Burtynsky was commissioned by Gerald Sheff and Shanitha Kachan to revisit the Point William site in 2018-2019 and reshoot the entire project capturing the changing seasons.

**James Dow** is a photographer based in Edmonton, Alberta. After studying with notable American photographers Minor White and Ansel Adams, he established his career in architectural photography. Dow's photographs have been published globally. He is a member of the Royal Canadian Academy of the Arts (RCA) and he received the Royal Architectural Institute of Canada's prestigious Allied Arts Medal in 2005. James Dow played a significant role in the landmark exhibition Capital Modern: Edmonton Architecture and Urban Design 1940–1969 providing new photographs of the heroic buildings of this modern period. He has been photographing the buildings and landscapes of Shim-Sutcliffe for over three decades, and the work at Point William for two decades, capturing the evolving relationship between built form and landscape in their work.

**Scott Norsworthy** is a photographer based in Toronto and he holds an undergraduate degree in architecture from McGill University's School of Architecture and a Masters of Architecture from the University of Toronto's Daniels Faculty of Architecture, Landscape and Design. He has photographed projects for distinguished architecture and design firms across North America. His creative and professional work is published internationally and has been included in numerous prestigious exhibitions.

## ESSAYS

**Kenneth Frampton** is an architect, critic, historian, and the Ware Professor of Architecture at the Graduate School of Architecture, Planning, and Preservation at Columbia University, New York. Frampton is regarded as one of the world's leading architecture historians of modernist architecture. Frampton is especially well known for his writing on twentieth-century architecture, and for his central role in the development of architectural phenomenology. In 2018, Kenneth Frampton was awarded the Golden Lion for Lifetime Achievement at the Venice Architecture Biennale. Kenneth Frampton visited Point William while it was under construction and upon completion, writing about its contribution to place making in the Canadian landscape.

**Michael Webb** is the author and editor of numerous essays and more than twenty books on architecture and design, including most recently *Architects' Houses*, and a memoir, *Moving Around: A Lifetime of Wandering*. He is also a regular contributor to leading journals in the United States, Asia, and Europe. Born in London, Webb became an editor at *The Times* and *Country Life*, before moving to the US, where he directed film programs for the American Film Institute through the 1970s and curated a Smithsonian exhibition on the history of American cinema. He is a regular contributor to *The Architectural Review*, *Mark*, *The Plan*, and has written extensively for *Architectural Digest*, *Domus*, and the *New York Times*.

## GRAPHIC DESIGN

**Anita Matusevics** is a multi-disciplinary designer with more than twenty years of international experience. A trained architect, Matusevics has held many positions in the design industry including senior associate at Bruce Mau Design. She is the co-founder of Wonder Incorporated, a Toronto-based design company focused on design thinking, visual communication, architecture, and art. Her diverse creative collaborations include exhibition design for Toronto's Harbourfront Centre and New York's Guggenheim Museum, book projects with photographer Geoffrey James and artist Guiseppe Penone, environmental graphics for the office of Dutch architect Rem Koolhaas, furniture design with Niels Bendtsen, and the Book Machine performance for Antwerp's Laboratorium Project.